Communication Information

By
Linda Barr

Illustrated by
Ron Himler

Columbus, OH

The McGraw·Hill Companies

Photo Credits

53 ©CERN;
55 ©Sam Ogden/Photo Researchers, Inc.

SRAonline.com

Copyright © 2005 by SRA/McGraw-Hill.

All rights reserved. Except as permitted under the United States Copyright Act, no part of this publication may be reproduced or distributed in any form or by any means, or stored in a database or retrieval system, without the prior written permission of the publisher, unless otherwise indicated.

Send all inquiries to:
SRA/McGraw-Hill
8787 Orion Place
Columbus, OH 43240-4027

Printed in the United States of America.

ISBN 0-07-604478-5

4 5 6 7 8 9 MAL 10 09

Contents

Chapter 1
Plant Paper 1

Chapter 2
The Pony Express 9

Chapter 3
Dots and Dashes 16

Chapter 4
A Signal to the World 23

Chapter 5
The Code Talkers 31

Chapter 6
Amazing Grace 38

Chapter 7
Caught in the Web 45

Chapter 8
Smiling Robots 54

Chapter 1
Plant Paper

Paper is becoming less and less necessary in our modern world. People used to send letters in the mail, but now many people send e-mails instead. Newspapers are still good places to find information, but more and more people are reading the news on Web sites. Businesses once used tons of paper, but now they do the same work on computers.

Yet computers sometimes crash, and files can be lost, destroyed, or inaccessible. Information on paper is safer.

Long ago, there was no paper. It hadn't been invented. People couldn't write the stories they heard or the things they learned; instead they had to remember everything. Imagine how hard that would be!

To record their ideas, people carved or painted pictures on cave walls, stone tablets, or other hard surfaces. However, carving in stone isn't easy, and people couldn't carry these pictures with them if they had to leave the area.

The ancient Egyptians solved this problem by making papyrus from plants. Papyrus is flat and lightweight, so it's easy to write on and carry. To make papyrus, the Egyptians sliced plant stems into strips and pasted together the strips. Then they stacked three layers of strips, soaked them in water, pressed them, and let them dry.

The word *paper* comes from *papyrus,* but papyrus isn't really paper. Papyrus is made up of stems pasted together. If you look at papyrus closely, you might see the stems.

A man from China named Ts'ai Lun invented paper similar to what we use today. About 1,900 years ago, he cut bamboo and tree bark, mixed them with water, and pounded them into a soft mush, or pulp.

Ts'ai spread the pulp, let it dry, and pressed it into a flat, smooth sheet. This paper was possible to make and easy to carry. In time, people around the world learned how to make paper. They tried using different plants, such as straw, silk, and seaweed. Some of these plants were more dependable than others.

The Chinese didn't only write on paper. They were the first to use paper as money, and they also used paper to make windows, umbrellas, toys, and many other things.

You can make paper in almost the same way Ts'ai did. Ask an adult to help you follow the steps on the next two pages.

How to Make Paper

To make a screen, bend a coat hanger into a square, and slide it into old panty hose.

Tear two newspaper pages into pieces. Half fill a blender with warm water and some of the paper, then close the lid, and have a responsible adult turn on the blender. Continue to add water and the rest of the paper to make a thick pulp.

Plug a sink, pour in the pulp, and mix in two tablespoons of white glue.

Slide the screen under the pulp, and slowly lift it, letting the water drain through.

Spread the pulp in an even layer on the screen, let it dry, and then carefully peel it off. Ask an adult to iron the dried pulp so it's flat. You have made paper!

Chapter 2
The Pony Express

If you wrote a letter on paper to someone today and sent it in the mail, it would probably take a day or two to get to its destination. But in the early 1800s there was no convenient way to carry mail across the United States, and delivery time for mail was weeks or sometimes months. Why did the mail system take so long?

The United States was not as populated then as it is now. There were vast, nearly inaccessible areas with no roads and no easy way to get from place to place. Stagecoaches and trains were used on roads and train tracks, and steamboats were used where there were no roads. Mail carriers often had to go long distances out of their way to deliver the mail.

When gold was discovered in California in 1848, pioneers began moving farther west. Getting mail from the East to the West and back again was difficult, and many Californians began to feel isolated from the rest of the world. Mail was delivered to California one of two ways. The first was by stagecoach, which was supposed to take twenty-four days, but instead it often took months.

The second option was to put mail on a ship that sailed south around the United States to Panama, then put it onto a train that crossed Panama, and then put it onto another ship the rest of the way to the West Coast. This process could also take a month or more. A more feasible solution was needed, and William Russell was the man who thought of it.

In 1860 Russell came up with the idea to put people on horses and send them across the country to deliver mail. Many people thought this was impossible because of bad weather conditions year-round, but Russell persisted. The Pony Express's first trip began on April 3, 1860, in Missouri, and arrived in California just ten days later.

One rider would ride his horse for ten or fifteen miles and then would change horses at a station to continue his journey. He would travel between seventy-five and one hundred miles in one day before another rider would take his place to continue across the country. Pony Express riders had to travel 1,800 miles from Missouri to California.

The mail was carried in saddlebags riders carried as they rode. Riders could weigh no more than 125 pounds, because the filled saddlebag weighed 40 pounds, and the horse could carry only 165 pounds total.

The Pony Express stayed in operation a little more than a year. It was discontinued in 1861 when the next great communication invention—the telegraph—was created.

Chapter 3
Dots and Dashes

The invention of the telegraph drastically changed the United States mail system. No one at that time had phones or computers, and a handwritten letter could take weeks to be delivered, even if it was carried by the Pony Express.

Imagine that you live in New York City in 1837, the time before the Pony Express. You send a letter to your cousin in San Francisco, with whom you have a close friendship.

Your letter will travel by train and stagecoach. The trip is very long—it might take months. If your cousin writes back, you won't receive the letter for a very long time.

This method of mail delivery was something people had to live with in the early 1800s. But a great change was on the way. The same year this old delivery system was still being used, Samuel Morse invented the telegraph, which sends an electric signal over a wire.

Morse's telegraph system works like this: Holding down the telegraph key a short time sends a dot. Holding down the key longer sends a dash. Morse wrote a code of dots and dashes; for example, "dot-dash" means the letter A. A telegraph operator uses this code to spell words.

In 1838 Morse demonstrated to people how his code worked, but few people cared. They didn't understand how useful it could be.

Six years later the first telegraph line was laid from Washington, D.C., to Baltimore, Maryland—a distance of only forty miles. Morse sent the first message over the new line using his code. This time people noticed. Morse code could change their lives! For the first time it was possible to send messages that would arrive the same day. People loved the idea.

More telegraph lines were laid, mostly along railroad tracks. Railroad stations sent telegraphs to one another to communicate when trains arrived and left.

Soon people in the towns near the railroad tracks began to use the lines. These people had been isolated from many of their loved ones before, but now they could easily communicate with friends and family who lived far away.

Citizens in the towns far from railroad tracks soon wanted to send telegraphs also. This meant new stations had to be built in order to reach these faraway towns. Additional, brand-new towns began to pop up near the newly built stations because people wanted to live near the telegraph.

Soon people in Europe wanted to send telegraphs too. In 1847 the first telegraph line was laid in Europe. Many more lines followed.

Sending a telegraph was actually quite easy. You went to the station, an operator typed your message in Morse code, and off your message went.

The long-awaited first transcontinental telegraph line was laid in 1861, finally connecting the East and West and eliminating the need for the Pony Express. When the telephone was invented in 1876, Morse code and the telegraph fell into the background as well.

Chapter 4
A Signal to the World

Martha Coston was destined for leadership. She was born in 1826. When she grew up, she helped invent a system of communication that would eventually aid the United States Navy. During a time when few women worked outside the home, Coston was working hard at developing her invention.

Coston's husband, Benjamin, was also an inventor. Sadly, he died when she was just twenty-one years old. One day Coston found some drawings her husband had been working on, and she realized he had been designing an idea for a new signal light called a flare. He thought if ships were in trouble or needed to communicate, the ships could use this flare to signal one another or to signal people onshore.

This took place long before computers or telephones were invented, but some ships were starting to use Morse code. Before he died, Coston's husband had been ready to test his new light. Coston decided to continue her husband's work and to carry out the test in his memory. Coston convinced the navy to test the flare her husband had developed. Unfortunately, the navy was unimpressed. They did not see a need for the flare.

Instead of giving up, Coston hired some men to help her experiment with the light. Coston and her workers experimented for ten years. She wanted to have red, white, and blue lights, each with a different meaning, but she and her workers were able to make only red and white lights.

Then one day Coston happened to see some fireworks with blue lights.

Coston wrote to the man who had made the fireworks. He couldn't help her create a blue light that was bright enough, but he did send the materials to make a green one. As a result, Coston was able to create three colors for her signal—red, white, and green.

In 1859 Coston got a patent for her lights. She put the patent in her husband's name.

Now that the lights worked reliably, the navy wanted to buy some to help its military ships signal one another. Coston set up a company to manufacture her ship signals. She also got a patent for her signals in several countries in Europe. Many European countries bought the patent from her so they could make their own lights.

After the Civil War began, the navy wanted to manufacture its own lights, so it bought Coston's patent for $20,000. However, it ended up costing the navy more to manufacture the lights on its own than to buy the lights from Coston. The navy decided to form a partnership with Coston and continue buying the lights from her. Yet Coston didn't get rich. To help her country, she charged the navy only for the cost of supplies.

When the war ended, the navy owed Coston $120,000, but they paid her only $15,000. Regardless, Coston's lights had helped win battles and save lives.

Coston's two sons eventually took over her company, which manufactured signal lights for one hundred years. Some ships at sea still use her lights.

Chapter 5
The Code Talkers

During World War II, the United States and Japan were enemies. When the American Marines sent secret messages to their military troops, they didn't want the Japanese to be able to read them.

Some people thought about using the language of the Native American Navajo as a secret code. The Navajo language isn't written; Navajo learn it by listening and memorizing. At that time, few other people knew the Navajo language.

Some Navajo showed the marines how the code could work. A marine would write a message in English, and then a Navajo would read the message and say the words in his own language. Another Navajo listened to the Navajo words and repeated the message in English.

Machines could send codes, but they took thirty minutes to relay the code. Besides, the Japanese were able to decipher most of the machines' codes.

The marines decided to use the Navajo code, and twenty-nine Navajo began training as code talkers. They made up an even harder code. Let's say a code talker said four Navajo words that mean "sheep," "tooth," "owl," and "pig." Then another code talker used the first letter of each of these words to spell another English word.

Can you figure out the word?

The code talkers also made up new meanings for Navajo words. For example, *besh-lo* means "iron fish" in Navajo, but the code talkers used *besh-lo* to mean "submarine." *Lo-tso* means "whale" in Navajo, but the code word *lo-tso* meant "battleship." *Dah-he-tih-hi* means "hummingbird," but in the code it meant "fighter plane."

The code talkers were sent to battlegrounds near Japan. There they helped send secret messages to American troops. Some messages told troops which way to go, while others warned that the enemy was moving in or of other dangers. In this way, the code talkers helped the marines win battles and saved many American lives.

In one battle, six code talkers worked for two days straight. They sent eight hundred messages without one mistake.

The Japanese heard the code talkers sending some of their messages. They had been able to break many codes, but not this one!

More than four hundred Navajo worked as code talkers, but their part in the war was kept secret.

The code was also used in the Korean War and the Vietnam War. No one explained how it worked until 1968, and now we know all about code talkers. We've learned how creative and brave they were. The code talkers have been given medals and awards for their service. They helped keep American soldiers safe and America's people free. They were true defenders of freedom!

Chapter 6
Amazing Grace

You've probably never heard of Grace Hopper, but she changed the world. Without Hopper, computers might not be as helpful as they are today.

Hopper was born in 1906. Airplanes had just been invented, and the first cars were being built. No one had even imagined computers.

Hopper studied math in college. Back then, few women went to college, and even fewer studied math, but Hopper was one of a kind.

Hopper became a college teacher and later joined the navy. There she started working with a computer—one of the first in the world.

This computer, called Mark I, wasn't at all like computers today. Mark I weighed five tons and was fifty-five feet long! With 760,000 parts combined, it was one of a kind, just like Hopper.

To make the computer work, Hopper punched holes in a strip of paper and sent the strip through the computer. The pattern of the holes commanded the computer, giving it specific tasks to do.

Mark I could do some mathematical problems, but it could store only seventy-two words at one time. How many words do you think a computer can store today? Billions!

When the first computers broke down, Hopper helped fix them. Once when she found a moth in one computer, she said the computer "had a bug." Since then, computer problems of any sort have been called bugs.

Hopper not only named computer bugs but also created a language called COBOL. COBOL controls computers with words, not numbers. Hopper designed ways for computers to communicate in words.

Some people thought COBOL couldn't work, but Hopper proved otherwise. She illustrated how companies could use COBOL. For example, COBOL could help companies send bills to customers. COBOL made computers more useful to the average person.

Before COBOL, a person had to know a lot of math to use a computer. Now people just have to know words to use a computer.

In 1966 Hopper retired from the navy at age sixty. She had helped make computers much smaller, more powerful, and more common. The next year the navy asked Hopper to work on a small project—and she worked for nineteen more years! During that time she became the first woman admiral, which is one of the top ranks a person can be in the navy. After those nineteen years Hopper retired again for good. She had earned it.

Hopper died in 1992. She had received many awards over her lifetime, but she received no patents, because there were no patents in the computer field at that time. Today there are millions of computer patents.

Hopper's intelligent work made it easier to use computers, changing our lives. She was truly amazing.

Chapter 7
Caught in the Web

While Grace Hopper was making computers easier to use, others were inventing the Internet. By 1983 the Internet was in use. The Internet links computers all over the world, creating a network of computers. It lets people send and receive files and e-mails as well as search for information. But in 1983 it wasn't easy to find information on the Internet.

Today when we want information on something from a computer, we enter the topic into a search engine and pages on the topic come up. Back then there was no way to do a search. You had to enter the name or address of each and every file you wanted. If you didn't know the name, you were out of luck. Using a computer to get information wasn't very easy or much fun!

Tim Berners-Lee made the Internet more useful and more fun. Berners-Lee was born in England in 1955. In 1980 he was working for a company that owned many computers. It was hard for everyone in the company to share files. Berners-Lee solved that problem by figuring out how to connect information together. This was the beginning of the World Wide Web.

As part of the Web, Berners-Lee invented two languages, HTML and HTTP. Have you seen those letters before? HTML names the pages on the Web. HTTP allows the Web to send the pages from computer to computer.

Berners-Lee invented a browser to help people find these Web pages. Two browsers we use today are Internet Explorer and Netscape. These browsers allow us to "surf the Web."

Many Web sites have information on the same topic, and some sites are linked to others with similar information. To allow people to jump from one site to another, Berners-Lee used hypertext—usually one or more words displayed in blue or black and underlined. If you click on hypertext, the computer will jump to another Web site. It's quick and easy!

In 1991 Berners-Lee put the first Web site on the Internet. Now millions of people around the world use the World Wide Web every day to send mail, get information, do business, shop, have fun, and experience the world.

Before the Internet was developed, daily life was much different. For instance, when students had to do research to write papers for school, they went to the library and found books to help with their research. Today it's still important to read books, but the Internet has nearly as much useful information and is easier to get.

Berners-Lee's invention has made millions of lives easier. You might think he must be incredibly rich. Although Berners-Lee has received many awards, he has received no money. He invented the Web for free and holds no patents on it. He wanted everyone to be able to use it freely. Now Berners-Lee is looking for ways to make the Web even more useful.

Chapter 8
Smiling Robots

Do you think a robot can feel happy or sad? Can it understand how you are feeling? Believe it or not, Cynthia Breazeal is building robots that act like they have feelings. Breazeal's first robots were just heads with many moving parts. If you spoke kindly to one, it would smile; if you yelled, the robot would bow its head sadly.

Breazeal worked with a company in Hollywood to make her latest interesting robot, named Leonardo. Leonardo is two and one-half feet tall and furry. He is not designed to walk; instead he has a "smart" brain. Inside Leonardo are sixty small motors; thirty of these make Leonardo's face move.

Breazeal is programming Leonardo to "understand," or interpret, how people feel. You can recognize how people feel by looking at their faces, right? Soon Leonardo will be able to do that too. Leonardo can already understand directions and carry them out. For example, if you tell him to push a button, he will. When you point, he looks where you're pointing.

Soon Leonardo will be able to know from your frown that he has made a mistake. If Leonardo doesn't understand you, he will look confused so you know you must repeat your instructions. In these ways, Leonardo will communicate with people and build relationships by copying and interpreting human emotions.

Of course, not all robots are like Leonardo. Some do basic jobs such as painting car doors in a factory twenty-four hours a day. Other robots do very dangerous jobs such as going into buildings to find bombs.

These robots can do only one job. They cannot learn a new job or understand what people tell them, but Leonardo can.

Breazeal's robots are designed to interact with people and learn from them. These robots are much more "humanish" than other robots. Because of this, Breazeal's new robots have many potential uses, such as helping people who can't move around easily. The person could tell the robot, "Please bring me a glass of water," and off the robot would go!

These robots could also help people who have difficulty speaking and therefore are unable to tell the robots what they need. To ask for help, these people could instead use hand signals the robot would understand. If a person felt sad, the robot would interpret the person's expression and understand that too.

Breazeal's robots are taking communication in a new, exciting direction. What do you think other future robots might be like?

Kids with Great Ideas

By
Hilary Mac Austin

Illustrated by
Lyle Miller

Columbus, OH

Photo Credits

7 ©Raymond Kleboe/Getty Images, Inc.

SRAonline.com

 SRA

Copyright © 2005 by SRA/McGraw-Hill.

All rights reserved. Except as permitted under the United States Copyright Act, no part of this publication may be reproduced or distributed in any form or by any means, or stored in a database or retrieval system, without the prior written permission of the publisher, unless otherwise indicated.

Send all inquiries to:
SRA/McGraw-Hill
8787 Orion Place
Columbus, OH 43240-4027

Printed in the United States of America.

ISBN 0-07-604477-7

4 5 6 7 8 9 MAL 10 09

Contents

Chapter 1
Louis Braille 1

Chapter 2
Chester Greenwood 9

Chapter 3
Margaret "Mattie" Knight 17

Chapter 4
Frank Epperson 25

Chapter 5
Krysta Morlan 34

Chapter 6
Kavita Shukla 43

Chapter 7
Two Brothers 52

Chapter 1
Louis Braille

What would we do without inventors? They make our lives easier, and they make our lives more enjoyable. There are many famous inventors, but did you know it's possible for children to be inventors too? It's true. Children have accomplished many important inventions.

For example, have you heard of braille? Braille is writing for people who are blind. Louis Braille invented this system of writing.

Louis was only fifteen years old when he invented this sensible, ingenious writing. The writing system is in patterns of raised dots, and blind people "read" and distinguish these patterns with their fingers.

Louis was born in France in 1809, and he was three when he became blind. When he was ten, he went to Paris to a special school for people who were blind.

Because Louis couldn't use his eyes, he learned by listening and memorizing, but he wanted to read books too. At that time there were only a few books for people who were blind. These books had raised letters that were very large, which meant the books were humongous and heavy. It was almost impossible to read and finish these books quickly; it took a long time to read just one sentence.

One day a man came to Louis' school in Paris. The man had invented an admirable new kind of writing for soldiers that helped them read messages that weren't visible at night. The writing was raised dots on paper, with different patterns of dots standing for different sounds. The writing was a special code the man called "night writing."

The military decided not to use night writing, so the man thought of using his invention for people who were blind. Unfortunately, the students at the school didn't like the writing. It took too long to finish a sentence because the sounds in just one word took up too much space. Also, the code was terribly difficult to memorize.

Louis also didn't think night writing was feasible, but he was intrigued by the concept and began to create his own writing. He used patterns of raised dots, but the dots didn't stand for sounds and weren't shaped like letters. Instead, Louis invented an alphabet of ABCs in which all the letters were patterns of raised dots.

In the braille alphabet each letter is represented in a rectangular shape that resembles a domino. Each rectangle can have up to six raised dots, and each letter is a different pattern. Louis also created special patterns for numbers and punctuation marks. He even created patterns for writing music. This was incredible!

Besides his system of writing, Louis also invented a machine that prints braille. This machine, called the Raphigraph, made it possible to produce an incredible number of books in braille. Louis was tremendously advanced and ahead of his time. People all over the world continue to use his writing system even today.

Chapter 2
Chester Greenwood

Sometimes inventions are simple, and you might think, "Wow, *I* could have thought of that." For example, who thought of earmuffs? Chester Greenwood did, and he was only fifteen years old! Greenwood lived in Farmington, Maine, in 1873. The winters are terribly chilly in Maine, and Chester's ears wouldn't stay adequately warm. His ears would become cold and numb whenever he went outside.

One year Chester received a new pair of ice skates, and he couldn't wait to try them! He dressed to go out in the frigid winter air, wrapping his scarf over his ears. But the scarf didn't do a very good job, and Chester's ears became overwhelmingly cold. He wasn't having any fun, though he wasn't willing to give up and go inside just yet.

Chester decided to solve his problem. He formed two circles of wire and asked his grandmother to sew fur onto each circle. Then he attached a band between the circles. The band went across the top of his head and held the fur over his ears. He tested his sensible invention and was astonished: It worked!

Chester's ears remained warm! He called his invention "ear mufflers" because a scarf is also sometimes called a muffler. Today we say simply "earmuffs." Chester patented his invention, and later he adapted and improved it. Every head is a different size, and Chester wanted to make earmuffs that would fit every size. He also wanted to make his earmuffs easier to carry.

Chester created a new, adjustable headband that could be made longer or shorter. These new stylish earmuffs could fit every size of head. This is what "one size fits all" means. What an imaginative idea!

Chester went on to create another sensible improvement for his invention.

Chester made the steel in the headband coiled. That way, when the band went across the head, the band uncoiled and fit tightly. When the earmuffs were taken off, the band curled again and overlapped itself. Now people could keep their earmuffs in their pockets because the earmuffs were collapsible. These improved earmuffs were not only adjustable to every head, but they were also easy to carry.

Chester later named his earmuffs Greenwood's Champion Ear Protectors. He opened a factory, and as earmuffs became more popular, the factory grew. Chester relished inventing and kept at it as time went on. Overall, he invented a folding bed, a hook to lift doughnuts when they're still hot, a new spark plug for cars, and a rake with steel teeth.

However, Chester is most famous for his wonderful earmuffs. People's ears are warm in the winter, thanks to Chester's imagination.

People in Farmington are especially proud of Chester. Every December the town has a big parade to celebrate Chester's incredible accomplishments. During the parade, everyone in town wears earmuffs—even the dogs. There are also gigantic earmuffs for the police cars!

Chapter 3
Margaret "Mattie" Knight

Margaret Knight was another child inventor. Mattie was born in 1838, and she grew up in Manchester, New Hampshire. Mattie loved to build things. People called her a tomboy because back then only boys were supposed to like to build, but Mattie didn't care. Neither did her brothers, because Mattie built the most admirable sleds in town!

Mattie's family wasn't rich, so when she was ten years old, she went to work in the textile mill where her brothers worked. Because of this, Mattie didn't finish school. This wasn't unusual; many children didn't finish elementary school back then because they needed to earn money for their families. Overall, Mattie and many other children worked thirteen hours a day at the mill. It was hard and dangerous work.

A textile mill is a place where machines weave cloth; these machines are called looms. One important part of the loom is the shuttle, which holds the thread and moves back and forth across the loom very quickly. Some shuttles in the mill had pointed ends, and it was dangerous when a loom broke down because the shuttle could come off the loom.

One day at the mill Mattie saw a horrible accident. A shuttle became loose on a loom and flew away from the machine, injuring a young worker. Mattie knew something had to be done. She had to fix this problem. She wished to make it so the shuttle would stay attached to the machine and so the machine would stop automatically when something went wrong.

Mattie made time after work each day to plan a way to achieve this. First she thought about what had to be done, and then she drew some sketches. Finally she built small models of her sketches. When she was done and the invention worked, she was quite pleased, and so was everyone else at the mill.

The invention was a stop-motion device, which means it automatically turned off the loom and stopped the shuttle from moving when something went wrong. Mattie never patented what she had accomplished; she simply gave her idea to the mill, because she wanted people to be safer as soon as possible. Soon her invention was being used in mills all over the country. And she was only twelve years old!

Just as Chester Greenwood continued inventing things throughout his life, Mattie continued to invent things as well. She patented almost thirty inventions including a special machine that created paper bags. The bags folded flat to make them easy to store. They also had flat bottoms so they were easy to carry and could hold more groceries. Then something astonishing happened—someone stole Mattie's idea!

In the end, Mattie had to go to court to prove she invented the paper-bag machine. She won her case. Mattie went on to invent machines that cut and sewed leather for shoes. She also invented parts for engines. She was a busy, responsible woman! She used her imagination, and she always had another new idea.

Chapter 4
Frank Epperson

Here's another great invention: the Popsicle! Many people love Popsicles because they taste great and keep us cool. Frank Epperson invented the Popsicle in 1905 when he was only eleven years old. You might think inventing the Popsicle would have been easy, because the Popsicle is just a frozen fruit drink. Anyone could have invented the Popsicle, right?

Actually, it was harder than you might think. In 1905 people didn't have the advantage of refrigerators or freezers to keep food cold or to make ice. In the winter, people cut ice from rivers and lakes and put the ice into a special container they called an icebox. Even with an icebox, it was hard to keep things cold because the ice always melted.

Frank Epperson lived in San Francisco, California. It doesn't get very cold there, so people there used to import ice from far away. If Frank didn't have ice or a freezer, how did he invent a frozen treat?

There are two versions of the story. The first version is that Frank's invention was a mistake: He stirred up a drink and accidentally left it outside overnight.

The second story is that Frank knew what he was doing. He liked inventing new fruit drinks, and one winter night he decided to try something original. He knew it was going to get miserably cold that night, so he left a drink outside with the stirring stick still in it. That night something incredible happened.

What was so amazing? It almost never freezes in San Francisco, but that night the temperature dropped below freezing. This was fortunate, because Frank's drink froze with the stirrer still in it. The next morning he removed the frozen treat from its container. He licked the treat, and it tasted good! But Frank couldn't do anything about his invention, because he couldn't figure out how to freeze something except by leaving it outside in a dish.

When Frank grew up, he married and had five children. He sold lemonade at fairs and amusement parks, but his family was still quite poor. Frank tried to think of ways to make more money. Then he remembered his frozen-drink invention. Making his frozen treat wasn't a problem because by then electric refrigerators and freezers had been invented. The time was right!

Frank thought his invention could be popular. He tried to find someone else who would manufacture his treats, but people told him his idea was misguided, wasn't feasible, and would never sell. That didn't stop Frank. He decided to do things himself. He invented a machine to freeze his treats, and he used test tubes as molds.

Frank established his invention and patented it in 1924. First he called his treat the Epperson Icicle, but too many people mispronounced the name, so he changed the name to the Epsicle. However, his children didn't call it an Epsicle—they called it "Pop's 'sicle." Frank liked that name better, so he renamed his treat the Popsicle.

At first, each Popsicle had just one stick. But in the 1930s many people were poor and couldn't afford Popsicles, so Frank invented the Twin Popsicle. The Twin Popsicle cost only a nickel and had two sticks, which meant that people could split it in half and share it. Frank later invented other frozen treats—the Dreamsicle, the Creamsicle, and the Fudgsicle— that many children still relish today.

Chapter 5
Krysta Morlan

Krysta Morlan is a young inventor in today's world. She invents things that help people with disabilities, and she has been very successful. Krysta was born with cerebral palsy, which means she can't use some of her muscles very well. Krysta's muscles sometimes spasm involuntarily, and this can make it hard to walk.

People with cerebral palsy sometimes have operations to improve their condition. When Krysta was in the ninth grade, she had a major operation on her legs. After the operation, she had casts on both her legs that went all the way from her hips to her ankles. She had to stay in bed while her legs were in the casts.

All summer Krysta recovered from her operation, and she was miserable. Her casts were hot. Her legs overwhelmingly itched all the time, and she couldn't scratch them. This was all extremely unpleasant, but Krysta didn't sit and cry. She decided to solve her problem. She thought about what would help her legs feel better in the casts. Krysta designed the Cast Cooler.

The Cast Cooler is an uncomplicated device made of a tube, a pump, and a battery. One end of the tube fits between the cast and the skin. The other end of the tube is connected to the pump. The battery runs the pump. Krysta used the pump from her aquarium because an aquarium pump normally pushes an overflow of air into water.

Krysta used the aquarium pump to send an overload of cool air down the small tube into her cast, next to her hot, itchy skin. The cool air inside the cast made her itch less and feel better, which was a lot more effective than just turning up the air conditioning.

The Cast Cooler wasn't all Krysta invented.

Eventually Krysta's casts came off, but her work wasn't finished. She hadn't moved her legs for a long time, and she needed special exercise, called physical therapy, every day to help her misshapen leg muscles learn to move, walk, and become flexible again. Even though she sometimes exercised in a swimming pool, it was boring, so Krysta decided to make it fun.

Krysta invented the Waterbike. Part of the Waterbike is above water, and part of it is underwater. The Waterbike works a little like a bicycle does, but it floats like a boat does. The person pedals the Waterbike like a bicycle, and the person's legs get the exercise they need. This is beneficial and effective therapy.

How does the Waterbike work? The pedals let the rider move the Waterbike around the pool, and a rudder makes it possible to steer so the person can control where he or she advances in the pool. The Waterbike also has fins for balance so it doesn't overturn. The whole bike is made of light plastic tubes and foam. This way the Waterbike doesn't sink!

The Waterbike is fun to ride, which helps make exercise fun. Physical therapy in the pool can feel like a game as the person pedals around in the water, all the while strengthening leg muscles and improving health.

When Krysta was a teenager, she became a successful inventor. Though she's older now, she continues to develop new ideas to help people with disabilities.

Chapter 6
Kavita Shukla

Kavita Shukla also lives in today's world, observing problems and thinking of ways to fix them. When she was thirteen years old, Kavita watched her mother pump gasoline into the car and then make the mistake of forgetting to put the gas cap back on the car afterward. Kavita saw a similar problem in her science class: Students continually forgot to put the lids back on bottles and test tubes.

The bottles had chemicals in them. Kavita imagined it would be very dangerous for scientists if they forgot to put the lids back on their bottles. If the bottles tipped over and chemicals were mixed together, there could possibly be a mishap and explosions. Kavita thought of a solution and invented a new lid. This lid reminds people to put the lid back on the bottle.

Kavita thought up a great name for her invention—the Smart Lid. If a scientist forgets to put the Smart Lid back on a bottle of chemicals, the lid beeps and lights. This reminds the scientist to put the lid back on, and the lab and scientists are safe from any potential explosions.

Kavita didn't stop there. She continued inventing, because she continued to see problems. The idea for Kavita's next invention came soon after she invented the Smart Lid. When she was in the seventh grade, she went to visit her grandmother in India. Some of the water in India isn't clean, and the bacteria can make people sick.

One day Kavita accidentally drank some contaminated water. She was afraid she would get sick, but Kavita's grandmother knew an old cure. She gave Kavita a spice called fenugreek. Fenugreek is often added to Indian cooking and is believed to kill bacteria. Kavita's grandmother's cure worked; Kavita didn't get sick.

Back home in the United States, Kavita wanted to find out how fenugreek works. She experimented and discovered that fenugreek works on water bacteria and on many other kinds of bacteria too. She also discovered that fenugreek works on molds. She learned that fenugreek makes some bacteria and molds grow more slowly.

One day Kavita took some strawberries from the refrigerator, but they were rotten. She was disappointed that the strawberries were inedible and was disappointed that the food had been wasted. *Too many people in the world need food for any to be misused,* she thought. Kavita remembered her experiments with fenugreek and wondered if fenugreek could possibly kill the bacteria that rot food.

She concocted a mixture of fenugreek and water, and then she added some paper, soaking it in her mixture. When the paper was dry, Kavita wrapped some food in it. Would the food rot as quickly as usual, or would the fenugreek in the paper help kill bacteria? The food stayed fresh longer! Food wrapped in her paper remained fresh four to six weeks longer than food without the special paper.

Without fenugreek paper

With fenugreek paper

Kavita's paper is natural, which is good for the environment; the paper is easy to manufacture, which is good for poor countries. The paper keeps food fresh longer, which is good for everybody.

Kavita received patents for her accomplishments and has also won many prizes. What will she think of next?

Chapter 7
Two Brothers

As you've learned by now, inventors can be any age. One boy was only eight years old when he invented something special for his mother. The boy's mother had a problem with her heart. Her heartbeat was too slow, so she had a pacemaker to help adjust the beats. A pacemaker is a small device that doctors put inside a person's chest.

A pacemaker has to be tested every week to make sure it's working properly and not destroyed. The boy's mother, however, didn't have to go to the hospital to do this test. Instead, she called the hospital on the telephone. The hospital tested her heartbeat over the phone! How is this possible?

Do you know about modems? Some computers use a modem to connect to the Internet. The boy's mother wore a special bracelet that could be connected to a modem as well. The bracelet read the pulse in her wrist and then sent her pulse electronically to a machine at the hospital, where doctors looked at the measurements.

Unfortunately, sometimes the bracelet didn't work dependably. The boy's mother had thin wrists, and the bracelet slipped frequently. This broke the electrical connection. The boy and his mother tried many ways to make the bracelet work better. The boy held the bracelet tightly to his mother's wrist, and his mother put water on her wrist. Water made the connection stronger.

Yet the bracelet still didn't work very well, so the boy decided to invent something better. He put an elastic band on the bracelet, which made the bracelet fit tighter. Then he attached sponges soaked in electrolytes. Electrolytes are special chemicals in our bodies—chemicals we need to stay replenished and healthy.

The boy had an electrolyte solution at his house that was for his pet lizard; even lizards need electrolytes. Why did the boy use an electrolyte solution? He knew electrolytes help with electrical connections better than plain water does. The boy's special sponges made the bracelet work more reliably. It was the perfect solution!

This eight-year-old boy had a brother who was six years old. The younger brother wanted to invent something as well. When he went to the hospital with his mother, he saw many patients who were young children. They didn't seem to be too delighted, and he wished to help them feel better.

When people are sick, sometimes they're given IVs. An IV is a way to give medicine; *IV* stands for *intravenous,* which means "into the vein." A bag of medicine is attached to a small tube, and the tube goes into a person's arm through a needle. Some IVs are hooked to tall poles with wheels so people can walk and won't be deprived of medicine.

The younger brother saw the children in the hospital walking with their IV poles, and he thought of an idea. His idea was to attach IV poles to small toy cars. This way children could ride around in the cars and receive medicine through their IVs at the same time.

These two creative, responsible brothers thought of delightful, helpful ideas. Many other children have ideas just as delightful. How about you?

Vehicles:
Getting from Here to There

By
Carole Gerber

Illustrated by
John Hovell

Columbus, OH

Photo Credits

Cover, Back Cover ©Gunter Marx Photography/CORBIS;
16–17 ©Royalty-Free/CORBIS.

SRAonline.com

 SRA

Copyright © 2005 by SRA/McGraw-Hill.

All rights reserved. Except as permitted under the United States Copyright Act, no part of this publication may be reproduced or distributed in any form or by any means, or stored in a database or retrieval system, without the prior written permission of the publisher, unless otherwise indicated.

Send all inquiries to:
SRA/McGraw-Hill
8787 Orion Place
Columbus, OH 43240-4027

Printed in the United States of America.

ISBN 0-07-604476-9

4 5 6 7 8 9 MAL 10 09

Contents

Chapter 1
Bicycles 1

Chapter 2
Trains 10

Chapter 3
Rowboats 19

Chapter 4
Canoes 25

Chapter 5
Sailboats 32

Chapter 6
Soap Box Derby Cars 39

Chapter 7
Planes 46

Chapter 8
Helicopters 54

Chapter 1
Bicycles

Every day motorists drive cars, bicyclists pedal bicycles, pilots fly airplanes, and sailors sail boats. But when was the last time you thought about what makes a bicycle's tires spin? What makes a helicopter rise off the ground? Transportation has always been an important part of society. This book will describe how vehicles work to get us from here to there.

Pretend you have taken apart a bicycle and laid all the metal and plastic parts on the ground. How many parts would you have? Would you have a dozen? Does the bicycle have a hundred parts? Would you count five hundred parts?

Would you believe these numbers are all too low? It's true! A bicycle has nearly 1,500 parts!

Bike riders don't need to know the purpose of every part, but it's important to know about the main parts.

A bike's largest part is the frame. The frame serves the same purpose as your body's skeleton: The frame manages to support the weight of the bike, just as your skeleton supports the weight of your body.

Your "frame" is made of bones. A bike's frame is made of steel or a type of plastic called fiberglass.

The frame is made up of three main parts—the front, the back, and the part you sit on. The front part hooks onto the front wheel. The back hooks onto the back wheel.

If the frame gets bent, the wheels can't turn properly. This can cause the bike—and its rider—to fall.

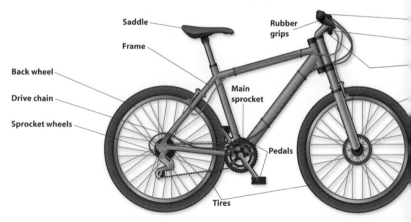

Handlebars attach to the front part of the frame. Handlebars should be narrower than riders' shoulders so bicyclists can comfortably hold the handlebars as they steer. Rubber grips on the handlebars help prevent riders' hands from slipping.

There are different kinds of handlebars for different needs. For example, racing bikes have low handlebars because racers bend over the bike as they ride.

——— Gearshift

——— Hand brakes
——— Handlebars
——— Front wheel

There are also many types of bike seats, which are also called saddles. Some riders like a long, narrow saddle, or a banana seat. Other riders find advantages in a wider saddle.

Nearly any seat will do for short trips. However, most racers who spend hours on their bikes and travel very long distances prefer a small, narrow seat.

What specific parts help a bike move? The pedals, bicycle chain, sprocket wheels, and tires all work together.

A rider's feet must first pump the pedals, which make other parts move. As each pedal moves, it turns a part that turns the main sprocket wheel. Small metal ridges, or teeth, on the main sprocket wheel fit into each link of the bicycle chain.

The bicycle chain, or drive chain, connects to at least one other smaller sprocket that hooks onto the back wheel.

When the drive chain moves, this makes the back wheel turn. When the back wheel moves, it pushes the bike forward, which makes the front wheel turn.

Some bikes have a gear system, which can make pedaling easier or harder. A gearshift on the handlebars allows the bicyclist to control the gears.

Pushing down on the gearshift makes pedaling harder, while pushing up makes pedaling easier.

Below the gearshift are hand brakes. Squeezing the hand brakes will make the bike stop. How can a rider stop a bike that doesn't have hand brakes? The rider must push the pedals backward.

It's fun to ride a bike. It's also fun to know what makes it work!

Chapter 2
Trains

Trains travel faster than bikes because trains have engines. Engines can give great power and speed to vehicles, and a train's engine is gigantic.

A train's engine is called a locomotive. The locomotive moves the train over railroad tracks, which are made of steel rails. The rails are held together by pieces of wood called ties.

Locomotives are built to help pull heavy loads. There are three main kinds of locomotive engines: diesel, steam, and electric.

Diesel engines are the most common and the most powerful. Diesel engines need diesel oil to work.

Steam locomotives have been around the longest. These engines burn oil or coal, which produces steam.

Most diesel and steam locomotives pull trains carrying freight. Coal, wood, food, and cars are all types of freight that trains transport from place to place.

Electric locomotives pull cars filled with passengers. Passengers are people who are traveling somewhere. In these trains, there are special passenger cars with windows, so people and tourists can look outside and watch the scenery go by.

Fast passenger trains are called bullet trains. For example, one particular bullet train in France can go 320 miles per hour! This train gets its electricity from power lines above the track.

The Eurostar is another electric train. This train carries hundreds of people to towns in Europe. Passengers leaving from London travel through the underwater tunnel known as the Chunnel.

Subway trains, such as those found in New York City and Paris, France, use electricity as well. These passenger trains travel underground through many tunnels. Passengers get on and off subway trains at different stops and take stairs to the streets above.

Electric engines are used for subway trains because steam and diesel engines produce dangerous fumes that cannot blow away underground.

You now know that a train is pulled by a locomotive. Behind this big engine is the line of public passenger cars or freight cars.

All the cars are connected together with hooks called couplers. The locomotive has a coupler on the back so a car can be hooked to it. Another car is hooked to the back of that car, then another is hooked to the back of *that* car, and eventually there is a long line of cars hooked together.

Extremely long trains often carry a lot of heavy freight. Power from two engines is needed to pull these loads, so sometimes two locomotives are hooked together at the front of the train. This doubles the power and allows locomotives to pull more freight.

Freight cars

Couplers

An engineer sits at the front of a train's locomotive. The engineer's job is to drive the train, and technology can make the job easier.

A computer shows if specific parts of the train are working. The engineer can make the train go faster or slower, switch tracks to reach a different destination, or stop.

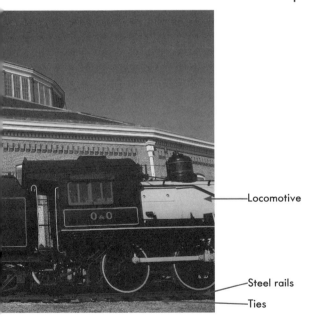
Locomotive
Steel rails
Ties

The yardmaster also has an important job. Yardmasters make sure trains don't run into one another. Technology helps with the yardmaster's job too; a computer shows the yardmaster what time each train leaves and which track it's on.

Yardmasters help prepare trains to carry freight or tourists by hooking and unhooking the cars. It takes many workers to run a train!

Chapter 3
Rowboats

When a boat is put in water, it will float—but only if the boat weighs less than the amount of water it replaces. If the boat weighs more than the amount of water it replaces, it will sink.

Enormous boats are called ships. They are extremely heavy, but they can float too. How? The boat has a lot of empty space inside, so overall it weighs less than the amount of water it replaces.

A boat in water will float wherever the current takes it. Current is the natural movement of water. If you stand at the side of a river and watch the direction the water moves, you're seeing the current. A boat will move with the current unless the boat is controlled and directed to overcome the current.

Rowboats are deep and wide, which makes them more stable than lighter, narrower boats.

A rower sits on a flat seat in the middle of a boat. To move the rowboat, the rower faces the back of the boat and pulls two long oars through the water.

The oars are held in place by metallic rings on the sides of the boat so the oars don't fall overboard.

These specific rings are called oarlocks. Oarlocks hold the oars in place as they dip into the water.

As the rower pulls on each oar, the oar pushes against the water, and the boat moves forward.

Rowing is easy to learn, but it can be exhausting if overdone, and it requires practice.

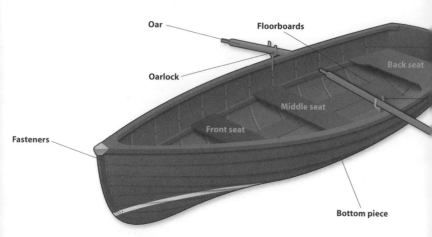

Most people rent or buy a rowboat that's already built. Others want to build their own boat.

To build a rowboat, you could cut oversize wood to the size you need, or you could purchase a rowboat kit.

Kits come with all the parts of the rowboat precut and ready to put together. Most rowboat kits include two sides, a bottom piece, floorboards, and front, middle, and back seats. The kit also includes fasteners, which are used to connect all the pieces of the boat.

Fasteners

Oarlock

Oar

If the boat is made of wood, the wood must be painted with an overcoat of waterproof paint. This ensures that the wood won't absorb water; the water will roll off the wood instead. If a rowboat's wood absorbs water, the boat will be heavier and will likely sink.

Chapter 4
Canoes

Rowboats are wide, bulky, and heavy. Canoes are narrow, graceful, and lightweight. Paddlers in a canoe face forward. They use only one paddle and hold it with both hands.

A rowboat's oars make a plopping noise as they push aside the water. A canoe paddle, if used correctly, hardly makes a sound at all. It cuts through the water, gently pushing aside the overlapping waves.

Today most canoes are made of aluminum or fiberglass. These materials float well and don't rot.

Older, classic canoes were made of wood, which is heavier and needs more care.

Canoes aren't as deep as rowboats, and this makes canoes easy to tip over. Rule number one is to keep your body low. Never stand up in a canoe—or you're likely to lose your balance!

If you lose your balance, you may fall overboard, which is why it's necessary to wear a life jacket at all times. You may still fall into the water and get soaking wet, but the life jacket will keep your head safely and effortlessly above water.

Having another person with you in the canoe is much safer, but paddling a canoe can be a tricky task for two people.

Here's an overview about how to paddle with two people. The two passengers should sit on opposite ends of the boat. The person sitting in the front of the boat, or the bow, holds the paddle on the left side of the boat.

The left hand should grasp just above the widest part of the paddle. This part of the paddle is called the blade. The right hand rests on the top of the paddle.

The right hand provides most of the power. The left hand steadies the paddle.

The other paddler sits in the back, or the stern, of the boat. This person's paddle goes into the water on the right side.

Here, the right hand goes just above the paddle blade, and the left hand rests on top of the paddle.

The paddler at the stern steers the canoe.

The paddler at the bow helps move the canoe by using smaller paddling strokes. The paddler in front also steers around rocks and other obstacles.

What if there's only one person in the canoe? Where would that person sit? In the middle, of course!

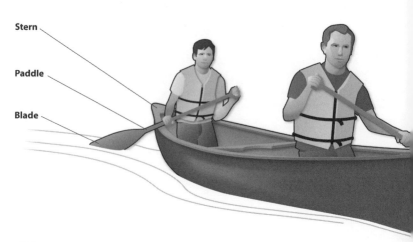

Using the correct paddle helps make canoeing safer, easier, and more enjoyable. Paddles are available in many specific lengths.

If you use a paddle that's too short, you may have to hunch over and hurt your shoulders. If you use one that's too long, the paddle may throw off your balance. Try several different lengths. Then put on your life jacket, make sure the canoe isn't overloaded, and paddle away!

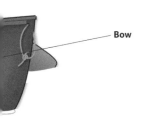
Bow

Chapter 5
Sailboats

Human muscle power moves canoes and rowboats through the water. A more natural force causes sailboats to move. This force is the wind!

Sailboats move when wind blows against their sails. When the wind blows overhead, the sails are pushed forward, which moves the boat.

The keel hangs along the bottom of the boat from the front to the back. The keel keeps the boat from being pushed sideways by the wind.

The largest sail is called the mainsail. The mainsail is attached to a pole called the main mast.

A small sail called the jib is in front of the main mast. The purpose of the jib is to help the boat change directions.

Some types of sailboats have two sails; other sailboats have more than two sails.

While only sailboats have sails, all boats share some of the same basic parts. For example, the main part of a boat that floats on the water is the hull. The hull gives a boat its shape. We've already learned about the pointed front of a boat, the bow. The pointed bow helps a boat move fast.

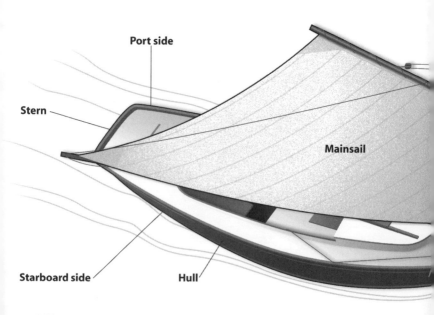

We've also learned about the back of a boat, the stern. The stern is rounded to help the boat easily overtop the water.

The left side of a boat is called the port side. The right side is called the starboard side. Sailors memorize all the parts of a boat and how each part works.

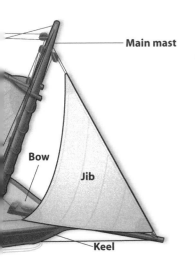

There are special smaller sailboats children can help sail. These sailboats are less than twenty feet long.

With only a mainsail and a jib, these smaller sailboats are fun to sail.

Of course, sailing is a skill that must be learned. There are many classes that teach children how to sail. You can learn how the parts of a small sailboat work and also how to keep a boat from capsizing, or overturning.

Many boats built for young sailors have terrific flotation compartments inside the boat. These are special small areas that keep out water and make the boat more buoyant, which means the boat floats more easily.

A small sailboat can capsize easily. If the boat does capsize, its flotation compartment can help the boat pop back up, and the water can be bailed out.

It's wise to test how well a boat floats before you sail it. Here's how to test it: Capsize the boat in shallow water.

Hold down the mainsail to see how long it takes the boat to overflow with water, and then see how quickly you can scoop out the water with small containers.

It should take only a few minutes to get a good boat upright and floating.

Chapter 6
Soap Box Derby Cars

Do you like to move exceptionally fast? Do you like to make things? If so, perhaps you'd like to build a wooden car and race it in the Soap Box Derby.

The Soap Box Derby is a race for children between ages eight and seventeen and is held each year in Akron, Ohio. The Soap Box Derby attracts boys and girls from all over the world.

The first Soap Box Derby experience was in Dayton, Ohio, in the mid 1930s.

Some of the cars were made from wooden boxes used to ship cartons of soap to the public. This is why the race is called the Soap Box Derby!

Today, the wooden boxes for shipping soap are no longer made, but the race cars are still made from wood.

Derby cars today still aren't allowed to have engines. Instead, the cars are able to move because the track they race on slopes downward very gently.

It works like this: If you're sitting on a skateboard at the top of a small hill and you push forward, the skateboard will pick up speed as you roll down the hill. Derby cars race on a track that's exactly 953.9 feet long.

Racers are required to build their own cars if they wish to race.

Cars built from special kits meet all the requirements for the Soap Box Derby. For instance, derby rules state that the weight of the car and the weight of the driver can't exceed a certain amount.

But even with a great car, it takes skill to win overall. The wheels must be perfectly aligned. Steering is important too.

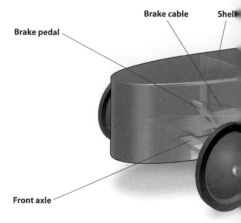

The important parts on a derby car are the floorboard (the bottom part of the car), the car shell, and the steering wheel.

To stop in derby-car traffic, a driver pushes expertly on the brake pedal, which is connected to the brake shaft with a brake cable.

The wheels are connected to the front and back axles.

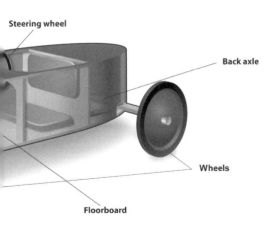

When racing, all drivers must remain in their own lanes, which is harder than you might think. The cars are designed so that drivers sit very low, and this makes it extra hard to steer.

However, sitting low helps with something more important: drag. Drag happens when overhead air hits the driver and slows the car.

The lower the racers sit, the less external drag there is on their bodies, and the faster the cars go.

Fast is good, but going too fast can be bad. The faster the car goes, the harder it is to steer straight. Cars that go outside the ten-foot-wide lane are disqualified from the race.

Most cars can go twenty-five to thirty miles an hour. Every fantastic second counts!

Chapter 7
Planes

As an airplane flies, wind pushes underneath its majestic wings. The wings have curved tops that affect how the air moves around them. These curves cause some air to flow over the wings and some to flow under.

The flat shape of the bottoms of the wings causes the air underneath to move slower than the air on top.

The slower-moving air beneath the wings pushes upward on the exterior of the plane. This pushing is called lift. Remember what happens when a sailboat's sails fill with wind? This is lift as well. Lift is also what helps a kite fly.

In order for air to blow over and under the wings, the plane must be moving. An engine is used to move the plane.

There are two important things the plane must overcome in order to fly. The first is gravity—which keeps everything on Earth on the ground—and the second is wind resistance.

To get off the ground, a plane must have lift equal to or greater than the force of gravity. This means that the air blowing against the plane must be strong enough to lift the plane's weight.

To allow the greatest amount of air to blow against the plane, the basic body of a plane is constructed to cause the least amount of resistance. If there is low resistance on a plane— if the plane is smooth and sleek— air will move easily across it. This way, the air has less to fight against as it lifts the plane.

The engines make the plane move. The engines have another job too: The engines control the propellers, which are spinning blades that extend in front of the engines.

When propellers spin, they pull the plane upward and through the air.

For the plane to land, the propellers must spin more slowly, so the plane can drop toward the ground.

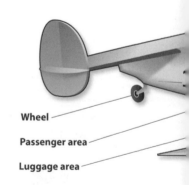

Wheel

Passenger area

Luggage area

There are also parts on a plane called flaps. The flaps are on the wings. When the flaps are raised, they create extra resistance against the air. This slows the plane when it is time for the plane to land. When a plane takes off, the flaps are lowered.

Landing and takeoff are the jobs of the pilot and the copilot.

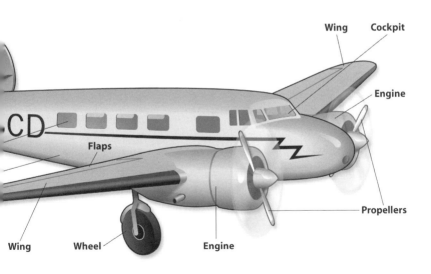

The copilot can also fly the plane if he or she needs to, but the pilot is the one in charge. Together, the pilot and copilot control the airplane's engines, wings, and tail.

The space where the pilot and copilot sit is called the cockpit; the cockpit is in the front of the plane. The cockpit has many automatic switches and buttons that control the plane.

There are buttons and switches overhead and even on the floor! The pilot and copilot use them all.

Behind the cockpit is the main area of the plane where the passengers sit and where luggage is stored.

The plane's wheels are outside the main area of the plane. They're small but important; without wheels, a plane couldn't land or gather speed to take off.

Chapter 8
Helicopters

Helicopters are amazing! They have thin propellers that spin around extremely quickly. These propellers, called rotors, lift helicopters into the air and enable them to fly in different directions.

Unlike planes, helicopters can fly backward. They can also fly up, down, left, and right, and they can hover without moving.

A helicopter's rotors are powered by an engine. The rotors are attached to a rotor mast above the cockpit, where the pilot sits.

When the rotors spin, they produce lift that quickly pulls the helicopter off the ground.

The pilot controls the main rotor, which determines the direction the helicopter flies.

The pilot also controls a smaller rotor on the helicopter's tail. This rotor steers the helicopter left and right.

Like an airplane pilot, a helicopter pilot depends on information displayed on various instruments in the cockpit. These instruments show the exact speed and height of the helicopter. Warning lights come on if any parts aren't working correctly.

Planes need to move quickly down a special stretch of road, or a runway, in order to take off, but helicopters can lift directly into the air.

However, helicopters are harder to fly than airplanes because of a mechanical system called automatic pilot.

Many airplanes have automatic pilot, which means airplanes can fly themselves for certain amounts of time—except for takeoff and landing—without the help of the pilot.

Many helicopters don't have automatic pilot. This means the pilot must always be focused on flying the helicopter, overseeing the instruments and keeping his or her eyes on the sky and on the land.

The pilot always keeps one hand on the collective control stick, an instrument on the floor that raises or lowers the helicopter.

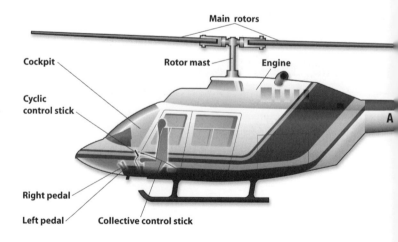

At the same time, this important instrument controls the amount of power coming from the engine. As the helicopter changes direction, extra power is needed to keep the helicopter moving at the same speed.

The pilot's other hand stays on the cyclic control stick. This instrument helps the helicopter turn side to side or move forward faster.

Tail rotor

In the meantime, the pilot's feet are busy pushing on two pedals on the floor that control the tail of the helicopter.

The pedals are a little tricky—pushing the left pedal turns the helicopter to the right, and pushing the right pedal turns the helicopter to the left.

It takes practice and extreme skill to fly a helicopter.

Uncle Teddy's Tale

By
Kathleen Thompson

Illustrated by
Lyle Miller

Columbus, OH

Photo Credits

36 ©Kevin Fleming/CORBIS.

SRAonline.com

 SRA

Copyright © 2005 by SRA/McGraw-Hill.

All rights reserved. Except as permitted under the United States Copyright Act, no part of this publication may be reproduced or distributed in any form or by any means, or stored in a database or retrieval system, without the prior written permission of the publisher, unless otherwise indicated.

Send all inquiries to:
SRA/McGraw-Hill
8787 Orion Place
Columbus, OH 43240-4027

Printed in the United States of America.

ISBN 0-07-604475-0

4 5 6 7 8 9 MAL 10 09

Contents

Chapter 1
A New Bicycle 1

Chapter 2
The Transcontinental Railroad 8

Chapter 3
West to East 14

Chapter 4
Uncle Maximilian 20

Chapter 5
Walking in the Dark 27

Chapter 6
Trains above the Streets 33

Chapter 7
The New Car 39

Chapter 1
A New Bicycle

"Uncle Teddy! Take a look at my new bike." I rode up to my great-uncle Teddy's front porch and managed to stop immediately in front of the steps.

"My goodness, Michael," said Uncle Teddy, smiling, "that's a fine bicycle!"

"I got it for my birthday. It's red!" I said proudly.

"I can see that," said Uncle Teddy. "It's as red as can be."

As soon as I got my new bike from the store, I pedaled straight over to Uncle Teddy's.

Uncle Teddy is my favorite person, and I knew he would probably be delighted about my bike. I was right.

Uncle Teddy encouraged my excitement, asking me all about the brakes and the bell. He kept repeating, "My, my, what a perfect bicycle!"

I parked by the stairs and climbed next to Uncle Teddy. I couldn't help myself—I turned around to admire my bike again. It was the same color of red as a fire truck. In my imagination I was a firefighter, full of courage and strength.

"When I was young, I had a bicycle that color," said Uncle Teddy.

I smiled. Uncle Teddy is always full of interesting stories, and I knew I was about to hear another one.

"You had a bike?" I asked as I collapsed into my favorite yellow chair next to Uncle Teddy in his rocker and prepared to listen.

"Of course I had a bicycle," answered Uncle Teddy. "My father was a railroad worker. He always managed to make good money for the family, so on occasion we could afford nice things like bicycles."

"Really? I thought maybe you had only a horse back then."

Uncle Teddy peeked at me over the tops of his glasses. "I'm old, Michael," he said sternly, "but I'm not *that* old."

"But you were born in 1919," I said, fiddling with the bandage on my knee. (I'd already fallen off my bike, and Mom made me put on a bandage.)

"And how do you know I was born in 1919?"

"You've told me a zillion times."

"You be careful, young man," said Uncle Teddy in a voice that let me know he was just teasing, "or you won't get pie." He had a twinkle in his eye, and I could see the reflection of my image in his glasses.

"Yes, sir," I said quickly. "I promise to be careful." Uncle Teddy's Mississippi mud pie was mouthwatering, and I would do just about anything to get some.

"Yes, I had a bicycle," said Uncle Teddy, removing his glasses and massaging the bridge of his nose. "My brother and my cousins all had bicycles, and my uncle Maximilian had a bicycle back in the 1880s in Denver.

"Back then our family didn't live here in Kansas City. Maximilian's father, my grandpa Nathaniel, made the decision to move out to Denver when the transcontinental railroad was built."

Chapter 2
The Transcontinental Railroad

"What's that?" I asked.

"The transcontinental railroad? Oh, that was tremendously important to the progress of transportation. It was important to the country, and it was important to our family," said Uncle Teddy. "The building of the transcontinental railroad was history. I suppose you'll want to know about that?" He smiled.

"I suppose so," I said encouragingly. I treasure Uncle Teddy's stories immensely.

Listening to Uncle Teddy's wonderful stories is better than watching television. He tells me about the old days when he was a boy and also about the days before he was born. Uncle Teddy is just about the best storyteller in our whole family. When Uncle Teddy has a new story for me, I always manage to find time to listen and learn.

"My grandpa Nathaniel was a skilled metalworker," said Uncle Teddy. "He could produce just about anything from metal. Even before the Civil War, Grandpa Nathaniel worked for the railroad, but the man who supposedly owned him got the money."

"Your grandpa Nathaniel was a slave," I said.

"He was a person who was forced to live in slavery until the end of the Civil War."

Uncle Teddy went on. "After the war, when Nathaniel was free, he continued to work for the railroad. He became an experienced worker in the metalwork profession."

"But he earned his own money?" I asked.

"He was free," said Uncle Teddy, "and that made all the difference. He was free and a railroad worker."

"The railroad started near the Atlantic Ocean, and then it moved west. First there were one hundred miles of track, and then there were one thousand. When the Civil War started, there were more than thirty thousand miles of track running through towns and villages."

"How do you know all this, Uncle Teddy?" I asked. I knew he wasn't alive when it happened.

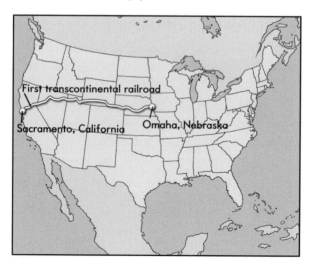

"My father was a railroad worker, remember? He told me all about the railroad."

"He told you stories?" I asked.

"I used to sit and listen to him just like you're listening to me. You can discover a great deal that way." He looked at me over his glasses with that same expression again.

"Yes, sir," I said. "I know that."

Chapter 3
West to East

"Out west in the United States, there were no railroads, so people walked and used stagecoaches—those were horse-drawn carriages," Uncle Teddy said.

"Then railroad workers started building a few tracks, but the tracks were only along the coast in California. At first they didn't build tracks that ran from the West back to the East."

"But how could people travel from one end of the country to the other?" I asked.

"They couldn't—not on the railroad," Uncle Teddy said. "Do you want some pie?"

"Not yet," I said, surprising myself. I really did want Uncle Teddy's pie, but I wanted to hear the story too. "What did people do?"

"The plan was simple. Workers started laying tracks for one railroad that began in the East and went west. The other railroad started in the West and went east."

"And they met in the middle!" I guessed. "Did they meet in the middle, Uncle Teddy?"

"They managed to come very close. The workers had to make a few adjustments at the end."

"That was a pretty big job, I guess. It probably took months," I said.

"A pretty big job?" exclaimed my uncle Teddy. He rocked forward in his chair and looked at me with piercing eyes. "Getting those tracks to meet was a huge accomplishment! Do you happen to know what lies between the east and west coasts of the United States?"

"A lot of land?" I asked.

"There are the Rocky Mountains, for a start," said Uncle Teddy. "It took six years and ten thousand people to build the transcontinental railroad. Sometimes they couldn't go over a mountain, so they had to blast a passage through the mountain rock with dynamite."

"And Grandpa Nathaniel helped?"

"He did," said Uncle Teddy.

"And then," Uncle Teddy went on, "Nathaniel moved from Chicago to Denver. He still worked for the railroad, and he married Grandma Elizabeth, who owned a very fine hat shop. They built a nice house on their own property, and Uncle Maximilian was born."

"And he had a bike," I said.

"You're jumping ahead," warned Uncle Teddy. "You miss a lot when you jump ahead."

Chapter 4
Uncle Maximilian

"What did I miss?" I asked eagerly.

"You go get us some of that pie," said Uncle Teddy, "and I'll tell you."

"But, Uncle Teddy—" I began.

"I'm sure I don't hear you arguing with me," he said as a motorist drove by.

"No, sir," I said swiftly.

Uncle Teddy kept rocking, and I went to the kitchen to get some pie.

I love Uncle Teddy's kitchen. Everything is old but also shiny clean. There are beautiful, ornate plates, painted by artists, on little shelves hanging on the walls.

He has a refrigerator he calls an icebox. Uncle Teddy uses lots of old words like *icebox.* The refrigerator has round corners and isn't much taller than I am.

I opened the refrigerator and proceeded to take out the milk.

I rummaged through the cabinet and took out two thick glasses and then got Uncle Teddy's tray. The tray is made of wood and has roses painted on it. I put the glasses on the tray and poured the milk.

Then I cut a humongous piece of pie for me and a significantly bigger piece for Uncle Teddy. Before I returned to the porch, I laughed at a cartoonist's comic in the newspaper on the counter.

"Here's the pie," I said, sitting down and swallowing a delicious forkful. "What happened next?"

"Well," said Uncle Teddy, "my uncle Maximilian was born in 1875, and he was extremely intelligent—smart as a whip. A perfectionist too.

"Maximilian proceeded to graduate from high school when he was only sixteen years old. People today usually graduate when they're eighteen."

"Wow," I said. "Your uncle Maximilian must have been very intelligent."

"Then he went to Oberlin College, in Ohio," said Uncle Teddy. "That was a long way from home for a boy."

"Is it?" I asked. "We went to Columbus, Ohio, last year. It took only a few hours on the airplane from Kansas City."

Across the street, a pianist began playing music in his house, and the song drifted out the window to our ears. It was very lovely.

"How long do you suppose it took my uncle Maximilian to get to Denver from school?" asked Uncle Teddy.

"On the train?" I asked, thinking Maximilian would probably travel on a train because his father was a railroad worker.

"Yes, on a train," said Uncle Teddy.

"Did it take him a whole day?" I asked.

The neighborhood florist walked by and waved hello to Uncle Teddy.

Uncle Teddy waved back and then held up two fingers to me. "It took Maximilian and his luggage two nights and two days."

"That's a long time!" I exclaimed.

"He couldn't go home for Thanksgiving or even for Christmas," said Uncle Teddy. "He didn't have enough vacation time to travel home and then back. How would you like that?"

"I wouldn't like it one bit," I said emphatically as another motorist drove by. "But I *would* like another piece of pie."

Chapter 5
Walking in the Dark

I returned to the kitchen and got more beverages and then sliced another enormous piece of pie for me and another for Uncle Teddy. Mississippi mud pie is so delectable and rich. I could eat an entire pie all by myself!

When I got back to the porch, Uncle Teddy's eyes were closed. I very timidly put down the tray. Then I sat and took my pie off the tray carefully and quietly.

"I'm not asleep."

I almost dropped my pie. My heart sort of jumped, and I twisted around.

"I was just resting my eyes," Uncle Teddy continued, chuckling at me.

Sure, I thought. "You were just trying to fool me."

"It worked, didn't it?" he said. Then he began laughing boisterously; it was contagious, and I proceeded to giggle as well.

"Do you know what my uncle Maximilian did after college?" Uncle Teddy asked.

"Did he become a dentist? A chemist? An artist?"

"No, he became a teacher. He went to the southern part of the United States because they needed teachers there. He taught in a country school that had only one room. He was very much admired and respected."

Uncle Teddy took a bite of pie. "The students came from villages that were miles away to go to Uncle Maximilian's school."

"How did they get to school?" I asked.

"They walked," said Uncle Teddy. "They walked three miles, sometimes four or five. Some children woke up at five o'clock in the morning and started for school in the dark."

"Their parents should have driven them," I said. "Children shouldn't have to walk that far. My parents would never make me walk to school in the dark without protection."

"But remember, people back then didn't have automobiles," Uncle Teddy said. "Most people didn't even have horses. Besides, the parents had work to do. You can't just leave a farm to itself in the morning."

"People who live on farms often begin work before the sun is up," continued Uncle Teddy. "A lot of them still work after the sun goes down. They manage to work even in the winter when there are frigid temperatures and snow is on the ground. It can be a difficult life for the whole family, not just the children."

Chapter 6
Trains above the Streets

"Was life like that for everyone?" I asked curiously.

"Life was like that for everyone who lived in the country. Cities were different.

"Grandpa Nathaniel and Grandma Elizabeth moved back to Chicago after Maximilian graduated from college, and my father walked to school, but he had an advantage: It was only a few blocks.

"I walked to school in Chicago too. It was so cold, I needed to bundle up completely," said Uncle Teddy. "But it was safer crossing the street back then."

"Why was it safer?" I asked.

"There weren't as many automobiles or motorists when I was a child as there are currently, and the automobiles that did drive by didn't go nearly as fast as the cars today."

"Did your family have a car?"

"Well," said Uncle Teddy wistfully, "that's another story. I can tell you if you'd like."

"Tell me the story!"

"A lot of railroad families lived in Chicago, just like my family did then," Uncle Teddy said. "On the way to their destinations, a lot of trains took passages that traversed Chicago. The Chicago train station was colossal."

"But did you have a car?" I asked.

"You're jumping ahead again. Be patient. Anyway, there's another kind of train in Chicago."

"This kind of train runs on tracks above the streets," he added.

"You mean *on* the streets," I corrected.

"I mean *above* the streets," said Uncle Teddy. "The train runs on tracks as high as a two-story building. The train goes all around the city on those tracks. It was originally called the elevated train; today people just call it the 'el.' It's really noisy!"

"But can people go places on the el?" I asked. This train sounded pretty extraordinary.

"Absolutely," Uncle Teddy said. "The el can take you to the stores downtown or to the pharmacist or to school. So, back when I was a child, people didn't need cars to get around the city, and lots of Chicagoans didn't purchase automobiles immediately."

"But the trains didn't take you out of the city, did they?" I inquired. "A car's advantage was that it could take you out of the city."

"That's what my father told my mother," said Uncle Teddy, his eyes crinkling. "Oh, that was something! Father wanted a car, and Mother didn't. Mother said we would all be killed, and Father said she was old-fashioned."

Chapter 7
The New Car

"Did your father win the argument?" I asked. I couldn't imagine a family without a car; it seemed so unrealistic.

"That's not exactly the way it happened," said Uncle Teddy. "After a while, my parents simply stopped talking about purchasing a car and becoming motorists. My father didn't mention the subject for weeks. In the meantime, we took the elevated train and walked to our destinations."

"Then one day my father came home from work. But he didn't arrive on the elevated train or in a carriage," said Uncle Teddy. "No, he drove up to the house in a brand-new car. And his grandmother was in it! Not his mother, you understand, but his grandmother. She was sitting there just as ecstatic and proud as she could be."

"What did your mother do?" I asked, grinning. I could just see Uncle Teddy's mother!

"What do you think she did? She got in the car!" said Uncle Teddy. "Nobody was going to think she was frightened. She was emphatic: If Great-granny could do it, my mother could do it too."

I was laughing very hard. "Did your mother ever learn to appreciate the car?"

"Of course she did," said Uncle Teddy. "Before long, Mother was as enthusiastic about that car as you are about your new bicycle. So was I.

"We became naturalists and went for relaxing rides in the country almost every Sunday afternoon in the summer. In the winter, we rode to church in comfort.

"And when that automobile wore out, we got another one."

"We also built a garage for the car. However, my father still rode the elevated train to work," Uncle Teddy added, "and I still walked to school and rode my bicycle to the park.

"In fact, my father didn't allow me to drive until I graduated from high school. But my family took some lovely vacations in that car. I still remember them. We had some rather fantastic times."

"And I'm going to have a fantastic time right now," I said. I got up from the yellow chair and gave Uncle Teddy a gigantic bear hug. "I'm going to ride my bike some more."

"That sounds perfect," said Uncle Teddy. "It's a wonderful day for riding a bicycle. Just as soon as you finish cleaning up these pie plates."

The Jumbled Journey

By
Becky Allen

Illustrated by
Robert Casilla

Columbus, OH

Photo Credits

35 ©Kike Calvo/Bruce Coleman, Inc.

SRAonline.com

 SRA

Copyright © 2005 by SRA/McGraw-Hill.

All rights reserved. Except as permitted under the United States Copyright Act, no part of this publication may be reproduced or distributed in any form or by any means, or stored in a database or retrieval system, without the prior written permission of the publisher, unless otherwise indicated.

Send all inquiries to:
SRA/McGraw-Hill
8787 Orion Place
Columbus, OH 43240-4027

Printed in the United States of America.

ISBN 0-07-604474-2

4 5 6 7 8 9 MAL 10 09

Contents

Chapter 1
Our Journey Begins..................................1

Chapter 2
Train Tracks to Naples...........................10

Chapter 3
Another Change of Plans....................19

Chapter 4
A Rain Forest Find..................................30

Chapter 5
Along the Amazon.................................37

Chapter 1
Our Journey Begins

For months our family had been planning an unforgettable trip to England with the Hamiltons. My name is Polly, and I have a younger brother named Josh. My best friend is Theresa Hamilton, and she has two older brothers named Tobias and Cameron. My parents and Mr. and Mrs. Hamilton and all the kids were going to England together!

At last the day to leave New York arrived. I was ecstatic with happiness. It was exciting walking through the airport on the way to our gate.

As we walked onto the plane, the flight attendant made an announcement: "Welcome aboard our 777!"

We couldn't believe our eyes. Our plane was huge!

"Let's find our seats," Mrs. Hamilton urged. "We're in the twenty-third row."

With four adults and five children, we filled a row of nine comfortable seats. Soon the engines roared, and the plane tore down the runway.
In six hours we would be in London. I wondered what I would do for six hours.

"Look!" Theresa said. She pointed to a screen hanging from the ceiling. "We can watch movies to pass the time."

"Not until you've had your lunch," the flight attendant said, placing trays with soup and a sandwich in front of me, Theresa, and everyone else.

"Yum!" said Tobias. "This is going to be an incredible trip!"

The hours went fast. Soon the plane landed in London, and we took a taxi to our hotel. I felt a great sense of awareness. I couldn't believe we were in England!

The following morning we were eager to explore. I couldn't wait to go to our first stop—the impeccable Buckingham Palace, where the queen of England lives. A real queen!

"The fastest way to reach the palace is on the subway. The British call the subway the tube," Dad explained.

I didn't know what to expect as Dad led us to a street corner and then down a staircase.

We were in an underground tunnel full of emptiness. Mom pointed to a map on the wall of possible train routes.

"Do you see how each subway route is a different color?" she asked. "We need to get on the green line."

Quickly a sleek, modern train pulled up, and we climbed aboard. Whoosh! The train immediately shot into the tunnel.

Soon we arrived at St. James's Park, which is just across from Buckingham Palace. On the way to the palace, something peculiar happened. Josh stumbled over a loose brick in the pathway. When he knelt to fix the brick, he found a flat, inexpensive tin box beneath it. Inside the box were a beautiful pin that looked like a butterfly and a handwritten note. Josh read it.

"'Please see that my daughter gets this gold pin,'" Josh read. "'Her name is Nora Banks, and she lives in Naples, Italy. I'm unable to send this to her. Thank you for your help.'" Josh looked up. "It's signed 'Joseph Banks.'"

What were we to do? It sounded like a fascinating adventure to me, even though it would mean a little craziness.

My parents and Mr. and Mrs. Hamilton talked for a short while. My mom had tenderness in her eyes, and I could tell she was considering taking the pin to Nora. After a few minutes, the adults looked at the children, and the children looked at the adults, and we all instantly knew—we were going to Italy to help Joseph Banks!

Chapter 2
Train Tracks to Naples

We decided to leave for Naples the next day and return to London later. To get to Naples, we first took a train to Paris, France.

"This train uses the 'Chunnel' to reach France," Mrs. Hamilton explained. "The Chunnel is an underwater tunnel. It passes under the English Channel."

I clapped my hands with happiness. We were going on an underwater train!

We filed into the train and found our seats. A young woman with a cart offered us snacks.

I began to get impatient, but before long the train entered the Chunnel, and the area outside the window turned black. We pressed our faces against the glass but saw nothing. I thought about all the water that must be floating around the tunnel walls and felt a little nervousness. Fifteen minutes later we reappeared in the daylight.

"We're in France!" Josh cheered. But we still had a terribly long way to go. The train started to go faster and faster. My dad said it was going 186 miles per hour!

When the three-hour trip ended, we bought tickets for our next ride. The trip from Paris to Naples would take more than fourteen hours in a regular train.

We stayed in private cabins on a night train and slept soundly in our bunks. The next day we were in Naples. I was so excited. The weather was beautiful, and the trees were very green.

We located Nora's address; she lived high above the city. A man on the street told us that Nora's home was inaccessible—except by funicular. What is a funicular?

The man pointed to the next corner, and we walked over and looked up.

"Look! The cars move along a cable," Tobias said. We watched the funicular climb the visibly steep hill. "Too bad it's inside a tunnel. We'd have such a great view."

We got on the funicular. I was glad we didn't have to climb steps instead!

Nora Banks owned an inn at the top of the hill. We introduced ourselves and explained that we had come a long way to find her.

When Nora saw the pin, she burst into tears. "My goodness, this is impossible. This was my mother's," she said. "Who gave this to you?"

Mrs. Hamilton told her about the box Josh had found and the note.

"My father had to give all his belongings to a nursing home," Nora said. "He had no other way to pay for his care."

"Your father must have loved you very much," my mother said gently. "The pin must have been special to him too."

Nora wiped away her tears and smiled. "I can't tell you how much this means to me. You've come such a long way. Won't you please stay for dinner?"

We did stay, and we ate homemade Italian spaghetti. It was indescribably delicious!

The next day we planned our return trip to England so we could continue our trip, but first we went to see some sights around Naples. We explored a castle, toured a museum, and shopped for souvenirs. In the middle of the afternoon, Cameron saw an elderly man sitting alone on a park bench.

"Are you okay?" he asked, approaching him. "I don't mean to be impolite, but you seem lost and full of sadness."

"I'm trying to get to Egypt," the man said. "My granddaughter needs my help."

We learned that the man—his name was Ahmed—had already traveled many miles. He was horribly tired and hungry, so the Hamiltons got him something to eat and offered him a bed in their hotel room.

That night we all agreed—we would travel to Egypt to take Ahmed to his granddaughter.

Chapter 3
Another Change of Plans

The next morning we went to the docks in Naples and climbed onto a ferry that would carry us across the sea to northern Africa. The ferry was a large white ship with three levels. It transported people as well as automobiles, small trucks, and bicycles. We sat on the top level where we could eat, relax, and enjoy the transportation.

When the ferry reached land, its horn bellowed with boldness. Then Mr. Hamilton gave an explanation about the next leg of the trip. "Now we have to cross miles of desert," he said. "And I thought a fun way to make the trip would be on the backs of camels!"

Our mouths fell open in disbelief.

"Wow!" Josh yelled, grinning. "I'm more than ready for that!"

It wasn't long before we found a guide with camels. The guide gave us each a cloth to wind around our heads and faces for protection against the hot sun and sand.

Then the camels knelt down for us to mount. As the camels plodded along, they swayed back and forth incessantly. "This is like riding on a boat," said Tobias, gripping the saddle.

My eyes began to hurt from looking at the sun's reflection on the bright sand. I looked at the camel's eyes—he had two sets of eyelashes! Pretty spectacular.

My mom threw a bottle of suntan lotion to me, and I put some on my arms and face. Miles and miles of sand stretched out before me. It was emptiness, but it was gorgeous!

At night we built a couple of fires and used them to cook our food, and then we slept in tents. The camels had carried our suitcases and supplies.

After many days of motion we finally arrived in the village where Ahmed's granddaughter lived. Ahmed ran to greet the impressive young girl. "These people have helped me find you," Ahmed said. "Now we can be together."

Before long, we bid farewell to Ahmed and his granddaughter. Then, instead of taking the camels back, we took a bus to the nearest airport.

We hoped we might return to England, but when we reached the ticket counter, something was wrong that needed our attention. Mom's suitcase was missing. She had picked up an incorrect bag—a bag that had a tag with an address of a person from China!

"This bag belongs to someone named Ping Chen," Mom said. "And I bet he has my bag."

"Quick!" Mr. Hamilton urged. "The next flight for Hong Kong leaves in ten minutes. To get your bag back, we need to return Mr. Ping's."

We dashed to the plane. In no time, we were jetting off across Asia. I laughed with happiness. This was some vacation!

When we arrived in Hong Kong, it was immediately humming with life. The air was full of conversation and vibration. Everyone seemed to be going somewhere.

We climbed onto a bus and then, later in the day, rented rickshaws, which are two-wheeled wagons that carry people. But instead of horses pulling the rickshaws, people on bikes pull them!

"I feel like a kid again," Mr. Hamilton announced with jubilation as he rode past us. "This is like riding on a big tricycle."

We sat in the covered cabs, enjoying the ride and the city buzzing around us. We passed many businesses and restaurants.

"What a great way to travel!" Theresa shouted gleefully. "Lots of fresh air."

In the tiny town of Li Pei, we found Ping Chen working in his yard. He and Mom were glad to get their bags back. Mom had missed her favorite shoes, and Mr. Ping had needed his robe.

That night we stayed with Mr. Ping. There was a celebration going on in town, and at first we were indecisive, but Mr. Ping convinced us to join the party.

There was a long dragon winding its way through the action in the streets. The costume was full of vivid colors, and the people underneath carrying the dragon were full of craziness! The dragon slithered along as if it were really alive.

We had a wonderful time, but the next day we were off on a train to the airport. We would try again to return to England.

Chapter 4
A Rain Forest Find

"This looks like something out of the future," Josh remarked as we climbed onto the maglev train. The modern white train sped to the airport at an incredible 265 miles per hour! But there were no wheels or engines. Powerful magnets lifted the train above the track and silently thrust it forward.

I giggled with Theresa. "Wow! This is like flying!" I said. She agreed with my opinion.

At the airport we stopped at a snack bar. The flight to England would be long, and we were famished. At the table next to us, a young woman seemed like she was in distress and suffering from dizziness. She coughed and wheezed, trying to catch her breath.

Mrs. Hamilton leaned over and gently asked, "Are you okay? Is there something we can do to help?"

"I'm sorry to bother you," the woman replied. "I have an unusual illness. The only cure is to drink a special kind of tea made from the leaves of a rare plant from the Australian rain forest. But I'm too weak to go find the plant. It's impossible for me to go that far."

Mrs. Hamilton sighed and turned to us. We all knew what she was about to say.

There was no doubt about it—
we were off on another vacation detour. We took a flight to an airport near the Australian rain forest and then rented two cars and drove north.

"I can't get used to riding on the left side of the road," Mom said.

"You should try steering from the right side of the car," Dad replied.

It really was strange to drive this way, but the views were too much of a distraction for me to notice. The highway to the rain forest stretched along the coast. The ocean was turquoise blue. Within a day we arrived at the edge of the rain forest. It was breathtaking, with millions of huge, glistening plants and the smell of wet soil.

To find the rare plant, we had to enter the heart of the forest. A guide suggested taking the Skyrail, which would carry us just above the treetops and then deep into the most inaccessible parts of the jungle.

Each family climbed into a small cabin that hung from a thick cable, and then we glided up the impressive mountain.

We caught an outstanding view of the valley and the sea below. As we swayed above the treetops, I slid open the cabin window. "Listen to all the amazing sounds," I said. "This place is really alive!"

Soon the Skyrail carried us to the forest floor, and we climbed out.

"Now search for a small red flower with five petals," Mom explained with determination.

Chapter 5
Along the Amazon

We crawled under shrubs and pushed back clumps of ferns. Soon Tobias squealed with delight. "I found some!" he yelled like a champion. We picked just the leaves of the plants and placed them into a mailing pouch.

On our way back to the Skyrail, I made a decision and stopped. I stood on the floor of the rain forest, looking around and thinking quietly to myself.

To think—just a few days ago I had been in New York, and now I'd been all over the world! I thought about all the cultures and lives that were so different from mine. They had made such an impression on me. All this because of a simple trip to England!

On the way back to the airport, we mailed the leaves to the woman in China, with the hope that they would help with her illness.

Before returning our rental car, Dad stopped at a gas station and filled the car with gas. A man at the station approached us with a panicked expression on his face.

"Please help me," the man begged. "My granddaughter in Brazil was injured in a fall and cannot walk. A doctor in New York can help her, but Taki has no way of getting there."

We had been traveling like crazy for days, but our incessant adventures had not ended. We were tireless! Our next stop was along the Amazon River in Brazil—the home of this nice man's granddaughter.

Once we reached Brazil, we had to cruise up the river to reach Taki's village. After a bit of discussion, two natives offered us a ride in their canoes carved from solid logs.

As the men paddled, we skimmed over the muddy waters, but it was hard work. We were moving against the current.

I looked for something to block the harsh sunlight, but the boat offered little comfort—not even seats. Instead, we sat cross-legged on the hard floor as the sounds of gurgling water trickled past us on our important mission.

Our voyage ended near a grove of rubber trees. I learned that the sap of rubber trees is used to make rubber.

"We'll need to ride mules for the rest of our excursion," Mom explained.

Our mules had no saddles or stirrups. Dad helped Theresa and me onto the animal's back. Mom rode behind us and held the reins as the mule walked to our next destination.

The mules carried us into the hills. It was a slow but steady journey. Cameron patted his mule's neck as it plodded along. "Sorry to load you down like this," he whispered.

I thought of the camels in Egypt and tried to make a decision. Did I like camels or mules better?

Within a few hours, we arrived at Taki's village. Her grandfather was filled with happiness.

Taki was waiting with an expression of disbelief. Her grandfather hugged her and lifted her onto a mule, and we all returned to the river, this time catching a large ship that carried us all the way to the sea, where we headed north toward New York—home! Taki and her grandfather made it to her doctor, but we never did make it back to England.

Am I sorry? Absolutely not! Our jumbled journey was wonderful! I've never had so much excitement on a vacation.

Contents

Chapter 1
The World Is Calling 1

Chapter 2
Why Is It Called a *Cell* Phone? 9

Chapter 3
Part Phone, Part Radio 19

Chapter 4
The Cell Phone Is Born 26

Chapter 5
Cell-Phone Awareness 37

Chapter 1
The World Is Calling

Imagine you're living before there was electricity—no TV, no radio, and no telephone. How did people communicate with one another before there were phones? Mostly they wrote letters to one another. Sometimes letters would take months to arrive, making communication extremely hard and slow.

Today telephones have become very important parts of our lives. We take for granted that we can immediately talk to someone by picking up a phone. Now that cell phones have been invented, our culture has changed quite a bit. It's possible to talk almost anywhere at almost any time.

In pre-cell-phone days, people could talk only on a phone that had a landline—a cord plugged into the wall. Inside the wall, a wire—or phone line—connects the landline phone to the rest of the system. Most people still have a landline phone, but they also have a cell phone.

Cell phones are a wireless improvement and can be used just about anywhere. People no longer have to stay in one place to make calls.

Landline phones were first used a little more than one hundred years ago in the late 1800s. At first only a handful of people had phones, and they could be used only in large cities because the lines connecting phones hadn't yet been prepared everywhere. However, as phones became more popular, new lines were constructed in more places, and about a hundred years later, phones were accessible to a billion people.

Cell phones have been catching on even more quickly. Only ten years after the invention of cell phones, a billion *more* people had these phones. Cell phones have become popular because they're so convenient and manageable. Because cell phones don't have cords, they work where landline phones can't. Now people can talk on the phone almost anywhere. Calls can be made and received from the side of a highway, from the middle of a lake, or from the top of a mountain.

In the United States about half the people own a cell phone. Many are even getting rid of their landline phones and choosing to use only cell phones.

In some European and Asian countries almost everyone has a cell phone. In these countries it's common for people to have no landlines—only cell phones. The reasons for this have to do with geography.

Landline phones are attached to wires, which are strung over land. In many places, running wires across the country is difficult and expensive. But cell-phone signals are sent through the air, and towers are used to send and receive the signals. These towers are simpler and cheaper to build than the structures needed for wires.

With the towers in place, communicating is much easier. There is wide agreement that the freedom to make a call anywhere is very desirable. This helps a country's economy grow, and people live better lives. For this reason and many others, cell phones are replacing many landline phones.

Perhaps you have a cordless phone at home. What's the difference between a cordless phone and a cell phone? Neither of them has a cord, so aren't they the same thing? Not quite. Cell phones are a little different from cordless phones.

Think about this: A cordless phone will usually work only at home—it's usually not possible for it to also work as close as next door.

This is because the cordless phone has to be close to a piece of equipment called a receiver, which plugs into the wall. The receiver connects the phone to the rest of the system. The cell phone, however, can be used wherever there's a signal—at home, next door, or in a different state.

Perhaps you're wondering how a cell phone works. It's very complicated.

Chapter 2
Why Is It Called a *Cell* Phone?

We'll start at the beginning. A cell phone is a two-way radio. One signal goes to a tower, and another signal goes from the tower to the phone. These independent signals let people talk and listen at the same time.

The tower is like the receiver for the cordless phone but much bigger. It takes calls from all cell phones in the area.

The area each tower covers is called a cell. Cell areas overlap so there are no gaps. This is where the name *cell phone* comes from!

A tower can take only a certain number of calls at a time (about fifty calls is the average), which is why cities need to have many towers. A big city needs an unbelievable number of towers to make sure cell phones aren't ineffective.

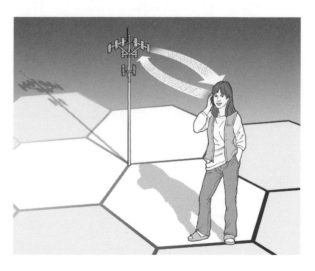

Cell areas can be bigger outside the city because fewer cell phones are used there. One tower in the country can cover many miles. Towers in the country environment are easy to see.

In the city, however, you may have the inability to see tower antennas because they're often on top of things that were already there, such as streetlights, flagpoles, and rooftops.

A cell phone is basically a radio that makes phone calls. Radios and landline phones, which send voices across long distances, are part of the cell phone's history.

Uncomplicated, sometimes incorrect forms of the telephone have been around for an unbelievably long time. One thousand years ago there was an incredible Chinese device historians think was a speaking tube.

Speaking tubes were used for hundreds of years. Have you ever talked into the end of a paper-towel roll? How does it make your voice sound? Speaking tubes work the same way. They run between the rooms and floors of a building or establishment. People who are far from each other can talk to each other indirectly and unseen through the tubes.

Another uncomplicated and inexpensive phone system used string stretched between two cups. When someone talks into one cup, it makes the string vibrate. The vibrations move through the string, and when the vibrations reach the other cup, the cup's shape amplifies the sound for the listener. The way the string carries moveable sound vibrations is similar to how an electric phone wire works.

A phone uses electricity to move signals along a wire. But the wire doesn't vibrate. Instead, the sound of a person's voice is used to change the way electricity flows in the wire. At the other end of the line, the changes are unscrambled back into sound.

Who invented the telephone? For years, innumerable historians thought it was Alexander Graham Bell.

Today historians know the inventor was an Italian named Antonio Meucci. In 1860 Meucci showed how a voice could be transmitted with electricity. But he didn't speak English; his discovery was written about only in Italian. Few people learned about it.

At this same time, other people were trying to show that it was possible to use electricity to send voices. But their devices were unsuccessful and ineffective.

Alexander Bell also was doing research and experiments. In 1875 he made a phone. A year later Bell made the first long-distance phone call to his friend, who was ten miles away! Bell brought his incredible device to the world's fair in Philadelphia. He didn't make the first phone, but he was the first to unveil it to the world.

Improvements were soon made to Bell's inconceivable telephone. Voices on the phone became clearer and louder, and wires were run all over the United States. In 1927 a call was made from New York City to London—over an entire ocean!

People were undeniably excited about telephones. But when did inventors first start to think about creating a cell phone?

Chapter 3
Part Phone, Part Radio

Today's phone system still uses wires to carry most calls. Landline phones send their signals through wires that connect to the phone system. But cell phones are radios, so instead they use something imperceptible called radio waves. Radio waves are invisible and move through the air, sort of like waves moving through water.

A radio transmitter is a piece of equipment that makes radio waves. But how do waves let you hear someone talking miles away? When a transmitter makes radio waves, the transmitter takes sounds—like the sound of your voice—and hides them in the waves. Then, when the waves are sent through the air, the sound of your voice is carried also. As improbable as it seems, your voice "flies" through the air!

As transmitters make waves, a radio receiver catches the waves the transmitter has sent through the air. Think of it this way: Imagine that you and your friend are standing in a big room. You write an important message to your friend on a piece of paper, and then you crinkle that paper into a ball. You throw that ball of paper across the room.

Your impatient friend catches the paper, uncrinkles it, and smooths it out. Your friend can now read the message you wrote. This is a little like how transmitters and receivers work, throwing invisible voice messages through the air on radio waves. This is also how cell phones work with radio waves—cell phones have both transmitters and receivers.

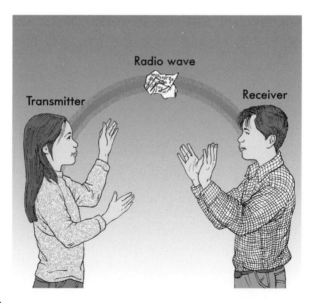

In the 1880s David Hughes created an instrument made of a battery and wires. He could turn electricity on and off in the wires, which meant he could make radio waves. Hughes saw that he could send sound signals with the radio waves.

He showed the device to other scientists, but they thought it was imperfect and didn't understand how it worked.

The other scientists thought Hughes wasn't really sending radio waves. They thought his device needed improvement, so they ignored his gadget.

In the next decade more devices like Hughes's were made, so it's unclear who actually invented the first radio. Some people think it was Nikola Tesla. He built a device in 1893 that worked just like radios people used years later. Tesla's device made a very great impact.

A few years later a man named Guglielmo Marconi built a radio that was like Tesla's. Marconi soon had an impressive factory making them, and for a long time many people thought Marconi invented the radio. But this story is like the story of Bell and the phone, because Marconi didn't invent the radio—he just independently unveiled it to the world.

Chapter 4
The Cell Phone Is Born

Ships were some of the first places where radios were used. People at sea could use the radio to communicate with those onshore, and this made ship travel safer. If something went wrong on a ship, it was possible for sailors to radio for help. Radios were good for talking to people on land, too, and for sending help over long distances. The world was becoming more connected.

In the 1920s police in Detroit put radios in their cars. These radios had an inability to send signals; they only received signals, which meant the police officers had to use phones to find out why someone had sent them a radio signal.

Soon police in other cities used these radios as well, and taxi drivers also found them helpful.

These first radios had a big problem. Signals crashed into each other. In 1927 a special group of people started making sure signals didn't crash.

Think of a highway. If there weren't lines on the road, people wouldn't understand where to drive and would crash into each other. In 1927 the special radio-wave group made sure radio waves traveled only where they were supposed to—through invisible road lines in the sky!

Another problem with the first imperfect radios was that they needed huge batteries.

However, during World War II in the early 1940s, the military created the walkie-talkie. The walkie-talkie uses small batteries and can be held in one hand. This technology was soon used in all radios.

Radios had many uses and helped many people communicate with one another. In 1946 the first dependable radios that could connect to the phone system were made.

But the special radio-wave group gave only a very small area in the sky to the radio waves for these radio phones. That area was much too small—only about twenty calls could be made at one time.

The idea for cell phones came from this problem. People had to figure out how to use that small, inadequate space in the sky to make many more than just twenty calls.

If you're really thirsty, do you drink just one tiny cup of water? No! You fill that cup over and over again. This is kind of how the scientists solved their problem. They figured out that to make more calls, they couldn't use each wave just once—they had to use the same waves over and over again. So, they made sure each tower in each area—or cell—reused waves.

Many responsible inventors worked on the idea of the cell phone. Then, in 1973, Martin Cooper made the first one.

In the 1980s cell phones were being used all over the world. People saw how impressive and convenient it was to always have a phone with them.

At the same time, phones were being made smaller. Then came digital code, which uses numbers to store lots of info in very small spaces. DVDs use digital code to fit movies onto small disks.

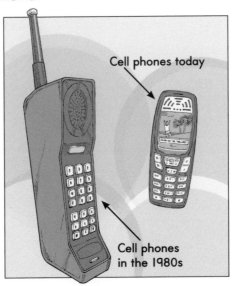

Radio waves carry a lot more info when they're in digital code. Cell phones that use digital code in their radio waves can send much more info.

The code allows cell-phone users not only to make phone calls but also to send text messages and photographs. The Internet and e-mail also are available.

Cell phones are becoming more like computers. Most cell phones have video games and can save phone numbers and addresses. Some phones even keep notes. Soon many cell phones will be able to show Web sites on their screens. It probably won't be long before you can watch TV shows and movies on cell phones too. Unbelievable!

Cell phones were once used only by businesses, but now it seems almost everyone has a cell phone. The smaller cell phones become, the easier they are to carry. If you go on a walk, you'll probably see several people with cell phones. Now try to imagine all these people carrying big landline phones. That would be silly, uncomfortable, and inconvenient.

People in the future might remember today's pocket-size cell phones and think *they're* too big! There are already phones that don't need to be held! How? Many cars today have hands-free phones. Drivers use their voices to command the phone to dial someone's number, and the incredible phone dials on its own.

Chapter 5
Cell-Phone Awareness

In 2002 researchers showed that a phone could be put in someone's tooth! My goodness!

When the person on the other line talks, the phone's tiny speaker sends the sound through the listener's face bones and into the ear. But this phone only receives calls—the user is unable to send calls.

What will phones be like in the future? How will this affect how we communicate?

Today the world buzzes with the sounds of people talking to one another on cell phones, sharing ideas, experiences, and happiness in places they could never use a phone before.

But cell phones are still a new part of our world. People are still finding out what cell phones are capable of. They're finding both problems and answers with cell phones.

For example, some places have decided that cell phones are too disruptive and cause unfairness to other people. These places sometimes use a new technology called a jammer, which blocks cell-phone radio waves. This means it's impossible for cell phones to work in these places. Some movie theaters and schools now use jammers so that movies and classes will not be interrupted.

Another problem is old cell phones. In just one year, more than fifty million cell phones were no longer needed by their owners. Almost 25 percent of those phones were put in landfills.

However, cell phones have lead and mercury inside them, which are poisonous. Recycling cell phones may be the answer to cleanliness—making sure these terrible poisons don't pollute the ground.

There are other answers too. Many phone companies take old phones and reuse the parts. Some charities take old, incompetent phones out of kindness. First they update the phones, and then they give them to people who are unable to afford to buy them. This way, many people are fortunate to have a phone with them at all times in case there's an emergency.

In spite of these problems, cell phones have truly changed the world. Many years have passed since the first telephone was invented. Can you imagine the craziness people then might have imagined when they heard about something that could let them talk with someone who was miles away? Today we talk on phones—with cords and without—every day.

If inventors could combine a landline phone with a radio and create a cell phone, what likeness might inventors come up with in the future to improve the way people communicate? Will cell phones get better and better, or will scientists think of something completely different that allows people around the world to easily communicate?

Maybe someone you know has a cell phone. The next time you see the person using it, remember your cell-phone awareness. Think about the considerable time and work that went into making that phone. Think how a voice is changed into radio waves and sent to someone's ears. Cell phones have become an important part of our culture. The whole world is just a phone call away.

Pen Pals Across the Pacific

By
Carole Gerber

Illustrated by
Oki Han

Columbus, OH

Photo Credits

6 ©Yang Liu/CORBIS.

SRAonline.com

 SRA

Copyright © 2005 by SRA/McGraw-Hill.

All rights reserved. Except as permitted under the United States Copyright Act, no part of this publication may be reproduced or distributed in any form or by any means, or stored in a database or retrieval system, without the prior written permission of the publisher, unless otherwise indicated.

Send all inquiries to:
SRA/McGraw-Hill
8787 Orion Place
Columbus, OH 43240-4027

Printed in the United States of America.

ISBN 0-07-604472-6

4 5 6 7 8 9 MAL 10 09

Contents

Chapter 1
Hello! 1

Chapter 2
What Is Your Family Like? 10

Chapter 3
Do You Enjoy School? 19

Chapter 4
What Do You Do for Fun? 28

Chapter 5
Favorite Foods 37

Chapter 1
Hello!

Dear Pen Pal,

Ni hao! My name is Li Ming, but my relatives and friends call me Mingming. *Ni hao* means "hello" in China, where I live.

I'm not sure how much you know about China. My teacher says I should tell you about it. In return, she says you might tell me endless things about the United States.

In China the government controls what people do more closely than in the United States. The government makes sure everyone has food and shelter. China is a little smaller in size than the United States, but our population is much bigger. About one billion people live in China—about four times more than the United States! I think life is very different here than it is where you live.

I've never had a pen pal. I breathlessly await your letter and would be very grateful if you wrote back!

      Sincerely,

      Mingming

Ni hao, Mingming!

I'm excited to hear from you and hope you can give me bottomless info about China. Why are you called Mingming instead of Li, since that name comes first? My name is Paula Franklin. I live in San Diego, California, and I have a brother named Dwight. What's the name of your city? Do you have any brothers or sisters?

                        Your pen pal,
                        Paula

Dear Paula,

In China, our last name comes before our first. My dad is Li Jun, and my mom is Wong Pei—women keep their last names after marriage. It is best for our country to have small families, so I have no siblings. I live in Kowloon. Tell me how to say your city—the letters are difficult and meaningless to me. I'm hopeful you can help.

Sincerely,

Mingming

Dear Mingming,

Here's how you say the name of my city: San Dee-a-go. San Diego is on the coast where it's gorgeous most of the time.

I like our zoo. In one part, the animals roam free in limitless areas. People ride in buses to look at animals wandering around. Do you have a zoo in Kowloon?

                Your pal,
                Paula

Dear Paula,

In Hong Kong's zoo, the animals are in cages. It would be interesting to see them roaming freely like in your zoo! Kowloon, too, is on the sea. I am enclosing a photograph of my city for you. Kowloon means "nine dragons," but there are no dragons—just harmless shops. I made a joke!

Sincerely,

Mingming

Dear Mingming,

Thanks for the photograph of Kowloon. There seem to be an endless number of bright, colorful lights everywhere! I wish I could visit your city. How big is Kowloon? I researched San Diego's population and learned that almost three million people reside here. Wow! I had no idea there were that many.

Your pal,

Paula

P.S. I liked your joyful joke!

Dear Paula,

I didn't know Kowloon's size, so my teacher told me to look on the computer. I learned that about two million people live here. It's big but not quite as large as San Diego.

There are many small, disconnected shops. As you can see, most shops have neon signs that flash ceaselessly and look really magnificent at night.

I've heard there are many cars in San Diego. Here there are not so many. Most people walk or ride bicycles. There's lots of sometimes reckless traffic—my teacher says Americans say "hustle and bustle." Kowloon is across Victoria Harbor from Hong Kong, where there are many successful banks. Kowloon has the shops. I love shopping. Do you?

                    Sincerely,

                    Mingming

Chapter 2
What Is Your Family Like?

Dear Mingming,

I like to shop too! I especially like shopping for clothes and toys, but I don't get to shop for them often. However, every week I go food shopping with my dad. We go to a big grocery store, and he always lets me push the cart. I get to choose my favorite healthful cereal.

Sometimes the people who work at the grocery store give free samples. Last week we tasted ice cream. Yum! Dad bought some to bring home. We also tried some cheese, but I disliked it. It was pretty tasteless.

I told Dad about all the bicycle riders in China. He said it would be good exercise instead of driving everywhere.

> Your pal,
> Paula

Dear Paula,

We buy food at shops in Mong Kok market. My grandmother and I buy chicken at one shop and then go to another for vegetables and fruits. We shop at bigger stores for clothes and toys.

My grandmother rides a bicycle. I love her very much, and I am very thankful for her. Does your grandmother live near you? What's your family like?

Sincerely,

Mingming

Dear Mingming,

Shopping with your grandmother sounds pleasant. It's so cool that she rides a bike! She sounds fearless! I'm not sure my grandmother knows how. I'll ask her when I see her. She lives far away.

I have to set the table for dinner, so good-bye for now. What do you look like? Please send a picture!

Your pal,

Paula

Dear Paula,

I asked my teacher what kind of picture you wanted me to send, and she said to send a photograph. That's what I have enclosed. My teacher said I should also tell you about my parents and their careers and other helpful facts. My father works for a hotel in Kowloon. My mother teaches at a nursery school.

My grandmother moved from the countryside to live with us after my grandfather died. She's been here since I was a baby and seems ageless. She walks with me to school, watches me while my parents work, and cooks dinner for us every night.

Please send a photograph and facts about your family.

Sincerely,

Mingming

Dear Mingming,

You look so pretty! Your parents and your grandmother look very friendly and delightful. I'm taking the picture to school to show my class.

We're having a family photograph taken soon. I'll send you one of those so you can see what we look like. I promise to write you more later!

Your pal,

Paula

Dear Mingming,

I'm writing again to tell you about my family. My dad's name is Jeremiah. He's a salesman. I think he's in his thirties. So is my mom. Her name is Anita, and she works part-time in a bookstore. My brother Dwight is six. Sometimes he's brainless but also funny. I'll send our picture soon!

                    Your pal,

                    Paula

Dear Paula,

Thank you for the wonderful two letters—they arrived yesterday. My parents are both thirty-six, and my grandmother is seventy-two.

It's nice that your mother works in a bookstore. My teacher says about 90 percent of China's people can read and write. She says literacy is important to our people.

Could you please describe your school?

Sincerely,

Mingming

Chapter 3
Do You Enjoy School?

Dear Mingming,

We finally had our family picture taken, and I'm sending one along with this letter.

My brother and I go to Tristan Elementary School. We really like the school. My dad says it's an excellent school that will prepare us for the future. Mom says my brother and I are very lucky to go there.

Do you like school?

Your pal,

Paula

Dear Paula,

Thank you for the photograph! Your family is extremely attractive. I like your brown eyes. Mine are brown as well. I predict that we will both grow up to be very beautiful.

I attend Li Cheng Uk Government Primary School. In China, students go to school six days each week. Sometimes it seems unfair and pointless to have to go to school so much. Do you go six days a week?

Sincerely,

Mingming

Dear Mingming,

You go to school six days a week? Wow! That's unbelievable. In the United States, we go only five days—Monday through Friday. It's pretty painless. We're in school six or seven hours a day. In elementary school, we have one main classroom teacher, but we also have teachers for music, art, and gym. I prefer math and dislike art. What's school like in China?

Your pal,

Paula

Dear Paula,

School is quite difficult in China. All students have six years of primary school. Then everyone takes exams to test their previous knowledge. Only about one-third pass and go on to secondary school. Students in big cities like mine have more courses and study the English language. Many villages have only primary schools. Grandmother says I'm lucky to live in Kowloon.

Grandmother went only to primary school in her village.

I work hard in school and expect to pass the tests I've prepared for, and then I'll go to secondary school for six years. My father says only 2 percent of students go to university. My parents expect me to go.

Science is my favorite subject.

Sincerely,

Mingming

Dear Mingming,

I read your letter to my parents. They say everyone here is offered twelve years of free school. Some people find jobs, but many students go on to college. The government tries to help everyone find the money to go to college, regardless of who they are, to make sure no one is prevented from going.

What do you do for fun?

Your pal,

Paula

Dear Paula,

Like many people in China, my parents and I like to fly kites. I learned in school that kites were invented about 2,500 years ago by Chinese people.

The frames that make the shapes of our kites are premade with bamboo, which is an almost weightless hollow wood. Then the bamboo is covered with silk cloth to form the kite.

I don't boast when I say that Chinese kites are the most beautiful in the world. I have several kites, and each is different. All are hand painted. My favorite is a butterfly. When families fly kites in the park, the sky is filled with displays of stunning silk creatures. I like to pretend they're alive!

Please write about what you and your family do.

Sincerely,

Mingming

Dear Mingming,

I love hearing about Chinese kites. It's so captivating! I hope you don't mind that I discussed your letter with my class. Everyone has asked if you'd send a photograph of one of your kites.

My family likes to surf. I'll tell you more about it next time. Right now I have to preheat a snack. I can't wait to see your kite!

> Your pal,
> Paula

Chapter 4
What Do You Do for Fun?

Dear Paula,

I'm delighted your class found the facts about Chinese kites to be so enthralling. I enclose a photograph of my favorite kite. It's 102 centimeters by 115 centimeters in size.

What does it mean to "surf"? That word is meaningless to me, and my teacher doesn't know what it means either. Tell me all about it, please.

Sincerely,

Mingming

Dear Mingming,

Your kite is awesome! My teacher says it's so beautiful that it should be hanging in a museum. It doesn't look tattered by the wind.

To surf, I stand on a special kind of board and "ride" ocean waves. I have to take precautions to stay safe, but still sometimes I lose my balance. It's fun to tumble into the water!

Your pal,

Paula

Dear Paula,

I don't think Chinese people surf, because I couldn't discover a word for "surf." My teacher said to explain to you that instead of words, we use special symbols called characters. Each character is like a picture. Each word has its own set of characters. There are thousands of characters, but I couldn't find one for "surf."

Here are the characters for "China":

                Sincerely,

                Mingming

P.S. Do you like music?

Dear Mingming,

I'm learning so much from you! Everyone in my class drew the characters for "China." Your way of writing is extremely different from ours!

Yes, I like music. I prefer playing an instrument called the viola that is similar to a violin but bigger. Do you play an instrument? If so, what kind?

Your pal,

Paula

Dear Paula,

Yes, I do play a musical instrument. It's like your viola because it's similar to a violin, but it's called an *erhu* and has only two strings. I know what a viola looks like. Can you imagine what an *erhu* looks like? Maybe you have seen one before. Musicians play *erhus* at our opera performances.

Sincerely,

Mingming

Dear Mingming,

No, I have never seen an *erhu,* but I went to the opera once. My teacher says opera is very popular in China because many of the stories tell about Chinese history.

I have a history question. Can you tell me about the Great Wall? I heard that astronauts can see it from space!

Your pal,

Paula

Dear Paula,

People here aren't sure if the Great Wall of China can be viewed from space. The Great Wall is about 6,700 kilometers long. That's approximately 4,200 miles, which is longer than the number of miles between the West and East coasts of the United States! People began building the wall more than two thousand years ago, and it took hundreds of years to complete. The Great Wall was built to prevent outsiders from entering China.

Sincerely,

Mingming

Dear Mingming,

Your letters are really interesting! I love learning about your culture and your life and how alike we really are.

You must practice your *erhu* a lot. I bet you play it effortlessly! I'm sure I'll never be asked to play the viola for an opera. I practice for only about fifteen minutes before dinner every night.

Speaking of food, what do people eat in 中国?

Your pal,

Paula

Dear Paula,

I'm honored to share facts with you about food in my country. Our main food is rice. In our southern regions, people eat rice for every meal. In villages everywhere, rice is all some people eat. In my family, though, we're fortunate to eat many types of food, including fish and vegetables. What foods do you like or dislike?

Sincerely,

Mingming

Chapter 5
Favorite Foods

Dear Paula,

I'm sending a second letter because my teacher said to tell you that our foods here have mostly five flavors: pungent, sour, sweet, bitter, and salty.

My family prefers small amounts of many foods. This is called dim sum. I think some restaurants in your country serve dim sum. Have you eaten this? I think it's very tasty.

Sincerely,

Mingming

Dear Mingming,

My family *loves* Chinese food and dim sum! When we order dim sum, the waiter brings a cart with a lot of choices. It's fun! My favorite is steamed dumplings with pork and shrimp. I can't remember the words for these. Can you remind me?

>Your pal,

>Paula

P.S. Here's a picture I drew of my favorite food!

Dear Paula,

The name for those dumplings is *sui mai.* I also like *sui mai.* Someday you should taste the cake made with turnips, called *lo bak go.*

Your hamburger picture looks delicious. I've eaten hamburgers at fast-food restaurants here, but my grandmother thinks fast food is tasteless. My father says some American guests at the hotel ask where to find fast food.

Sincerely,

Mingming

Dear Mingming,

My family prepares and eats most of our meals at home. When we have hamburgers, my dad usually grills them outdoors.

I told my parents about the cake you recommended. Mom says next time we order dim sum, we'll choose *lo bak go* for dessert!

What kinds of fast-food restaurants are in China?

Your pal,

Paula

Dear Paula,

We have all kinds of fast food. There are American fast-food restaurants that sell hamburgers and pizza, but there's also other fast food. Our fast food includes things like noodles, dumplings, and steamed bread. I disagree with my grandmother: I like to eat all kinds of fast food!

My family, like yours, usually eats meals at home.

Sincerely,

Mingming

Dear Mingming,

My teacher wants me to discuss how rice is grown and harvested in China. She says rice is a crop that grows in paddies. What are paddies? I told her you probably haven't harvested rice, but you said your grandmother lived in a village. Does she know how rice grows?

Write soon!

> Your pal,
> Paula

Dear Paula,

My grandmother lived in a village in south China, where endless amounts of rice are grown. She says my people have grown rice for more than five thousand years. She says rice is actually a kind of grass—I didn't know this! Rice is planted in paddies, which are shallow puddles. The paddies are drained before the rice is harvested.

Rice seedlings are planted one at a time by hand, spaced a hand span apart. (A span is the distance from thumb to little finger when the fingers are spread.)

Writing you has been so much fun, Paula! If you want, please continue to write to me. Who knows—maybe one day we can meet!

>Sincerely,
>
>Mingming

Storm Chasers

By
Kathleen Thompson

Illustrated by
Susan Lexa

Columbus, OH

The **McGraw·Hill** Companies

Photo Credits

Cover, Back Cover ©PhotoDisc/Getty Images, Inc.;
22 ©Jon Davies.

SRAonline.com

 SRA

Copyright © 2005 by SRA/McGraw-Hill.

All rights reserved. Except as permitted under the United States Copyright Act, no part of this publication may be reproduced or distributed in any form or by any means, or stored in a database or retrieval system, without the prior written permission of the publisher, unless otherwise indicated.

Send all inquiries to:
SRA/McGraw-Hill
8787 Orion Place
Columbus, OH 43240-4027

Printed in the United States of America.

ISBN 0-07-604471-8

4 5 6 7 8 9 MAL 10 09

Contents

Chapter 1
Crazy Ideas 1

Chapter 2
Why Chase Storms? 9

Chapter 3
All About Chasers 19

Chapter 4
The Warning 28

Chapter 5
The Storm 37

Chapter 1
Crazy Ideas

"Are you crazy?" I heard my dad bellow. His powerful voice boomed out of the kitchen and almost shook our old farmhouse. The cat looked up and then replaced her head on her paws. I just continued to read. Mom and Dad were having a silly talk. I wasn't worried.

They were talking about one of Mom's friends. She wanted to come visit, but Dad seemed to think Mom's friend was strange. He was saying he couldn't be comfortable with Mom's friend in the house, but I could tell he was kidding just a little. That's how my dad is.

"Dolores is my oldest friend," I heard Mom say.

"She's a storm chaser. She chases tornadoes. She's wild!" said Dad.

Mom laughed. "She's also a math teacher," she said. "And her husband is a science teacher."

Dad gave a hugely dramatic sigh. "Why would anyone want to chase a tornado?"

Chase tornadoes? That sounded really different and interesting! We live in Oklahoma, and there are lots of tornadoes in Oklahoma. Usually, though, people don't chase tornadoes—they run from them. Tornadoes are extremely dangerous, and you must be careful with them. I put down my book and went into the kitchen. "What's a storm chaser?" I asked curiously.

"Well," said Mom, "you know about tornadoes in Oklahoma."

"They're very dangerous," said Dad. "They cause a lot of damage."

"Yes, they do," said Mom. "Some people drive around this part of the country looking for tornadoes and other storms. They take helpful photographs and measure the storms," she explained.

"*They* think it's cool," said Dad, sticking out his tongue at Mom. "Normal people don't go after something so dangerous!"

Mom playfully poked Dad's arm. "You're not so normal yourself." Then she looked at me. "My friend is always very careful when she follows storms. She knows what she's doing and always returns unharmed."

I remembered that Dad's brother had once been in a tornado. Was this why Dad was acting so funny? "Uncle Luke was in a tornado, right?" I asked.

Dad's face instantly changed. He became serious, and Mom patted him on the back. "Yes, Rebecca," she said, "your uncle was in a tornado."

"It was really awful," said Mom. "Your uncle Luke and aunt Victoria lost nearly everything. The tornado destroyed the house, the barn, the car, and even the fences. Most of their belongings had to be replaced."

"The weather service issued a warning first, so Uncle Luke and Aunt Victoria went to the basement where it was safe," Dad said.

Chapter 2
Why Chase Storms?

Dad looked out the window at the surrounding fields. Western Oklahoma is incredibly flat, so you can see for miles from our house. "I hate tornadoes," Dad said. "They're dreadful. I don't think people should play with them."

"But the warning saved Uncle Luke," Mom said. "And storm chasers help weather reporters."

"Storm chasers don't just take photographs," said Mom. "They report tornadoes and learn how tornadoes build and rebuild. At least, my friends Dolores and Tony Sanchez do. They help the weather service save lives." Mom smiled at Dad. "You know, some people might say *you're* silly for working outside under the scorching sun all day."

"You're right," Dad said. "Dolores is your friend, so they can visit a while. But all they'll want to talk about is frightful tornadoes!"

"Then maybe you'll learn something," Mom said to Dad, and she winked at me. "I'll call Dolores."

Grown-ups are funny, I thought, and I returned to reading.

Mom telephoned Mrs. Sanchez and started giggling softly. Dad made a funny face at me and walked outside to do some work.

In bed that night, I thought more about storm chasers. It seemed unsafe to me. How could storm chasers safely chase tornadoes? I'd be frightened, but I suppose it would be exciting if I was careful.

Right before I fell asleep, I wondered what Mr. and Mrs. Sanchez would be like. What would they look like? Would they look like normal people? Or would they look different? I couldn't wait to talk to Mom's friends and find out all about storm chasers. Slowly I drifted to sleep.

A week later, the Sanchezes arrived in a small van. Mrs. Sanchez was small and plump, with bright, friendly eyes and a pretty smile. She scampered to our front porch and hugged Mom tightly. "Oh, you look wonderful!" she said, laughing and rehugging Mom. Mom was laughing too. She was happy to see Dolores.

Mr. Sanchez was tall with curly dark hair, glasses, and a shy smile. He walked up to the porch and shook Dad's hand meaningfully and then hugged Mom gently and said hello to me. Dad seemed surprised that the two of them looked so normal. I liked both of them instantly.

Mom walked the Sanchezes upstairs to the guest room, and Dad and I looked at each other as he started to laugh playfully.

"Why are you laughing?" I asked.

"They don't look how I thought they'd look," Dad said. "They look like you and me."

"What did you think they'd look like?" I asked.

He shrugged his shoulders. "I don't know. Like movie heroes or something."

"That's how I thought they might look too," I said. "They seem very friendly."

"Yes, they do," Dad said. "But they still do pretty strange things."

"Maybe there's a reason for that," I said.

"Maybe," he answered, shrugging again.

"Dad, have you ever seen a tornado?" I asked. He nodded. "What was it like?" I asked.

"It moved across the land like a powerful giant."

"A giant?" I asked. All I could imagine were two enormous feet dropping from the clouds.

"A giant," Dad said seriously. "Big and fast and hungry."

Chapter 3
All About Chasers

About an hour later, Dad went to work in the fields, and I went to my friend Rita's house. We played a fun game and then went out to a nearby field to look for old arrowheads. We were unsuccessful, however, and became disinterested. I returned home, where Mom and Mrs. Sanchez were on the porch playing dominoes and laughing.

I sat on the porch and asked Mrs. Sanchez lots of questions.

"How fast do the winds in a tornado blow?"

"The fastest tornado ever recorded had winds spinning at 318 miles per hour," Mrs. Sanchez said, restacking the dominoes. "Your car goes only 60 miles per hour, so 318 is pretty fast."

My eyes opened wide in disbelief.

"How close can you get to a tornado?"

"That depends on the tornado. We've discovered that sometimes we'll see one fifteen miles away, but it'll be sunny and pleasant where we are. If we get too close, it becomes dangerous." I thought about Uncle Luke and Aunt Victoria. That tornado came too close.

"Sometimes one large tornado can disintegrate into lots of smaller tornadoes," Mrs. Sanchez continued. "So we have to be really careful to watch where each tornado is moving. We always call the weather service to tell them when more tornadoes have formed. Then they can issue a tornado warning so other people know."

"Are you really scared when you chase tornadoes?" I asked.

Mrs. Sanchez grinned. "I know some people disapprove, but the reason I chase tornadoes is that they're so powerful and fascinating to watch. Sometimes I get nervous, but we're always very, very careful. If a tornado gets too close, Mr. Sanchez and I know exactly what to do."

"Do you dislike thunderstorms?" she asked me.

I shook my head. "No, I actually really like storms. I like when the rain pours, when the lightning lights and relights the sky, and the way thunder makes the whole house tremble."

"That's a little like why I enjoy watching tornadoes. Nature can be quite amazing," she said.

"Everything we learn is used to help people stay safe," Mrs. Sanchez said. "We tell people when a tornado is forming, we discover where and why tornadoes form, and we find the best ways to stay safe."

I wished Dad had been around to hear all this. I'd tell him later.

The Sanchezes left the next morning, but before they left, they showed me some of their storm-chasing tools in disorder in the back of their van: a laptop computer to get weather reports, radar, a camera, and a cell phone.

"We checked the weather this morning. We're lucky—the weather is perfect for tornadoes," Mr. and Mrs. Sanchez said gleefully.

"Lucky?" said Dad as they drove away. "They think it's lucky?" Then I retold him everything Mrs. Sanchez told me. He listened and was quiet. Then he looked at me and smiled sheepishly. "You know what? I was wrong for disagreeing," he said. "Maybe I was the foolish one!"

I was glad he understood.

Chapter 4
The Warning

At lunch, the radio reported a tornado watch, but it was no big deal because there are lots of tornado watches in Oklahoma in the summer. We're more mindful about tornado warnings. There's a big difference. A watch means a tornado might form, but a warning means there is a tornado.

After lunch, Rita came over, and we played outside. When it started to feel cooler, we returned inside.

Dad came in too. "It looks like a storm out there," he said. "The sky is almost black."

We looked out the window. The sky was getting darker and more discolored, and it was only four o'clock.

Rita and I listened to the radio. "A tornado watch is in effect," the reporter on the radio said. Still there was no tornado warning. The radio wasn't loud. In fact, it was becoming difficult to hear. Suddenly there were powerful noises that sounded like rocks hitting the roof. It was hail.

"I don't like this," Dad said.

"The radio hasn't reported a tornado warning," Mom said.

"I know," Dad said, "but I don't like it."

"Maybe I should go home," Rita said, moving her wheelchair toward the door.

"No," Mom disagreed. "You shouldn't go outside. Stay here. Your parents know you're safe here."

After a few minutes, the hail stopped, and even though it was very quiet, we could hardly hear the radio. We couldn't hear what the disintegrating voices were saying, so Mom turned it off.

"Is the storm over?" I asked.

"Let's just stay inside," said Dad. "It's better to be safe than sorry."

"This could be the calm before the storm," Mom said thoughtfully.

"What's that?" I asked.

"When a tornado is coming, there's a big storm, and then sometimes the storm stops, and it's very quiet. Then the tornado comes."

I looked out the window. The trees weren't moving at all. Was this the calm?

But minutes went by, and no tornado came.

Mom reconsidered. "I guess it's over. Don't you think so, Christopher?"

"I guess so," said Dad, and he got up from his chair. "I'll give you a ride home, Rita."

The two of them moved toward the front door, and then the telephone rang.

I picked up the phone. It was Mrs. Sanchez.

"Don't be afraid, dear," she said. "Just go to the basement."

"Why? What's going on?" I asked.

"It's a tornado," said Mrs. Sanchez. "It's moving toward you."

I turned away from the phone. "It's Mrs. Sanchez," I whispered in disbelief. "A tornado is coming right at us!"

I turned back to the phone and listened carefully.

"We're right in front of the storm," said Mrs. Sanchez. "We're close to your farm, and we'll try to get there, but you and your family must go to the basement now."

I hung up and retold Dad what Mrs. Sanchez had said.

Chapter 5
The Storm

Dad rushed to the basement door. "Come on, girls."

I hurried downstairs, and Dad carried Rita, while Mom quickly grabbed Rita's wheelchair and followed us. Then the cat came down. Dad closed the door, but he thoughtfully didn't lock it because he wanted it to be open for the Sanchezes.

Everything was silent, and then we heard the siren that meant there was a tornado warning. Suddenly the basement door flew open, and Mrs. Sanchez came down the stairs with Mr. Sanchez hurrying after her. Dad slammed the door and locked it. We looked at each other gratefully and sighed with relief.

We heard a noise like a train growing louder and louder. I grabbed Mom, and Rita started to cry, so Mrs. Sanchez hugged Rita.

"Don't worry," Mrs. Sanchez whispered to Rita.

We heard crashing. Suddenly the train noise disappeared, and it was quiet again. We all huddled in the basement, listening nervously.

It was over. Rita stopped crying, and Dad opened the door. We carefully crept up the stairs. Dad said he would be brave and go first. We trailed behind, and Mr. Sanchez carried Rita.

It was light in the house. It was too light. Then I knew—we were looking at the sky!

Oh no! The living room was gone! The roof, the second floor, and two walls had disappeared, and the TV was also gone. Later, we found the TV near the barn, a chair in my tree house, and a table in the garden. We were all very lucky that no one was hurt.

Of course, it was not all just luck: Mr. and Mrs. Sanchez had saved our lives. Dad was the first to say how grateful we were. "Thank you, Dolores," he said to Mrs. Sanchez. He started to say more, but he just hugged her. I think he was crying a little. I was crying too.

"Were you really close to the tornado?" I asked Mr. Sanchez.

"We saw it when it touched the ground, but we were far away, so we were safe," he said. "But then it began to move toward your house, and we were suddenly at a disadvantage. We started driving. It seemed to follow us the entire way."

"We got here just in time," Mrs. Sanchez said. "We called the weather service, and they started the siren."

I was extremely upset about our house but thankful we were okay. I was even a little excited that I had been in a tornado—but not too excited. One tornado was quite enough for me!

Contents

Chapter 1
The Ocean 1

Chapter 2
The Desert 6

Chapter 3
The Forest 12

Chapter 4
The Plains 18

Chapter 5
The Mountains 23

Chapter 1
The Ocean

The sun rises. It is the start of another day in the ocean. Tiny plants live on the surface of the ocean water. These plants are plankton. Plankton are like all living beings. They cannot live without energy. Plankton get energy from the sun.

A school of blue-green mackerel fish swims and looks among the plants. There are so many fish, the school is miles long and miles wide. The mackerel are very hungry, but they cannot get their energy from the sun. How do they get energy? They eat the plankton!

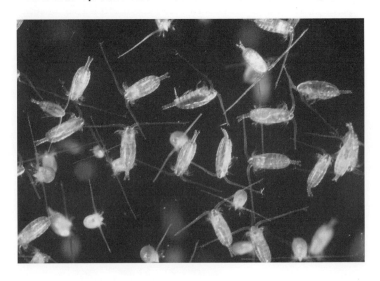

A striped tuna swims under the school of mackerel. It is larger than a mackerel. It needs even more energy. How does it get the food it needs? The striped tuna doesn't eat plants. It eats mackerel! The mackerel gives the tuna energy.

The tuna swims toward the school of mackerel. Food! The tuna darts quickly at its prey. It catches a mackerel. Breakfast!

A huge great white shark lurks nearby, keeping a lookout. It needs even more energy than the tuna. That means the shark needs even more food.

How will the shark get good energy? The shark will eat the tuna! The shark snaps its large jaws, and it catches the tuna. Gulp!

The sun feeds the plankton. The plankton feed the mackerel. The mackerel feed the tuna. The tuna feed the shark.

Chapter 2
The Desert

The sun sets. It is the end of another hot day in the desert. Now the sun is down, and it is cooler outside. The animals are waking up, and they are all hungry. A kangaroo rat has spent the day underground.

It is cool in the kangaroo rat's burrow during the day. Now it pokes its head out. Then it climbs out and scurries into the empty, rocky desert. It is looking for seeds.

A rattlesnake is asleep under a rock. At dusk it slithers out onto the cooling sand.

The snake senses the kangaroo rat, and it coils up its body. Suddenly it strikes! The rat tries to escape on foot. It leaps high into the air, but it is not fast enough. The snake bites the rat, and its fangs inject a deadly venom.

Then the snake swallows the rat in one big bite! The rat has succumbed to the snake. Now the snake is full, and it will not eat again until tomorrow. The snake's knowledge of where to look for the rat has paid off.

A red-tailed hawk flies into the starry night sky. It has sharp eyes. They help it see well at night. It looks down at the dry desert. It spies the rattlesnake. The snake is full of food, and it is moving slowly.

The hawk swoops down! It catches the rattlesnake with the talons on each foot. Dinner! The snake has given the hawk energy.

The seeds feed the rat. The rat feeds the snake. The snake feeds the hawk.

Chapter 3
The Forest

It is early springtime in the forest. One morning a caterpillar climbs out of its egg sac. It is on the leaf of a strawberry plant. This is perfect! During this first phase of its life, it must eat right away, and leaves are its food. Right away it starts munching on the leaf.

That night an opossum wakes up. She carries her babies in a phenomenal pouch, just like a kangaroo. Opossums sleep during the day and wake up at night.

Now that the opossum is awake, she must look for food.

The opossum sees the caterpillar on the leaf. She grabs the caterpillar with the sharp claws on her foot. She pops it triumphantly into her mouth, and then she walks away through the forest.

The opossum will search for food all night, and she will eat almost anything—even trash!

That same night a bobcat prowls through the dark, leafy forest. Its stomach is growling. It catches the opossum's smell in the moist night atmosphere.

The bobcat follows the smell, and soon it sees its prey. But it knows it must be silent or the opossum will get away. When it is near enough, the bobcat physically crouches down on its knees. Quietly it watches, and it gets ready for the right time. Then it pounces!

The bobcat is quick, and it is physically strong. It succeeds with the knowledge that it has caught its food.

The leaf feeds the caterpillar. The caterpillar feeds the opossum. The opossum feeds the bobcat.

Chapter 4
The Plains

It is summer on the plains. The hot sun shines on the tall grass. Gophers stick their heads out of the ground. A huge herd of buffalo eats the grass. They are big animals with shaggy hair. They eat grass all day long. They need to get fat before winter.

In winter there are not as many plants. The buffalo have less to eat. In winter the fat on their bodies helps keep them alive.

A group of Lakota Native Americans is camped nearby. In a way, the Lakota are like the buffalo. They are getting ready for winter too.

Of course, the Lakota are also different from buffalo. The Native Americans don't eat just plants. They eat animals too. And they cannot store as much fat on their bodies as the buffalo can. They have to find food and put it away for later. This food has to last all winter.

The Lakota need to gather a lot of meat. So they hunt the buffalo herd. The men move quietly into the herd on horses or on foot. They shoot at the buffalo with their bows and arrows. In triumph, they hit their target.

A buffalo falls to the ground. Then the women go to the dead buffalo. They cut up the buffalo meat and dry it. It is hard, physical work. Just one buffalo can feed many people.

The grass feeds the buffalo. The buffalo feeds the Lakota.

Chapter 5
The Mountains

It is fall in the mountains, and the leaves on the trees are changing color. A ground squirrel is looking for nuts and berries. It must work quickly! It needs to eat a lot of food. Winter is coming, and soon it will go to sleep. The squirrel sleeps all winter long!

Sleeping all winter is called hibernating. When animals hibernate, they breathe more slowly. Their hearts beat more slowly, too, during this phase. The animals don't eat. They just live off their fat all winter. Then they wake up in the spring. They are really skinny and hungry!

Nearby, a grizzly bear is also looking for food. It is seven hundred pounds, and it is eight feet tall! That is enormous! The grizzly bear knows it must find a lot of food for its big body. It needs to get ready for winter too.

The grizzly bear likes to eat nuts and berries, and it hibernates, just like the squirrel. The squirrel and the bear are a lot alike. But physically the bear is bigger. It needs a lot more food than the squirrel needs.

Nuts and berries are just not enough for the bear. It is still hungry. Just then, it smells the squirrel, and soon it finds the squirrel's burrow. The bear has sharp, curved claws. They are perfect for digging. It digs into the burrow. It catches the squirrel.

The berries and nuts feed the squirrel. The squirrel feeds the grizzly bear. This is called the food chain. Animals need to eat other animals, bugs, and plants for food. Life continues because of the food chain.

A Floating Town

By
Kathleen Thompson

Illustrated by
Arvis Stewart

Columbus, OH

Photo Credits

Cover, Back Cover ©Tibor Bognar/CORBIS.

SRAonline.com

 SRA

Copyright © 2005 by SRA/McGraw-Hill.

All rights reserved. Except as permitted under the United States Copyright Act, no part of this publication may be reproduced or distributed in any form or by any means, or stored in a database or retrieval system, without the prior written permission of the publisher, unless otherwise indicated.

Send all inquiries to:
SRA/McGraw-Hill
8787 Orion Place
Columbus, OH 43240-4027

Printed in the United States of America.

ISBN 0-07-604467-X

4 5 6 7 8 9 MAL 10 09

Contents

Chapter 1
Rainy Days... 1

Chapter 2
A Lot of Fish!... 6

Chapter 3
Living on a Boat 12

Chapter 4
Town Problems 17

Chapter 5
How to Fix It 23

Chapter 1
Rainy Days

Tonlé Sap is a lake in the country of Cambodia. It is a very big lake. Once a year, it grows and gets even bigger. When that happens, the people in the town of Kompong Luong have an issue. You will soon see why.

For half the year, Tonlé Sap is almost as big as a small state in the United States. Then rain falls for many months. The lake fills up and gets much, much bigger. Soon it is more than four times as big as before. Amazing but true!

Think about that. Is there a lake near your school? Are there houses near the lake? Or stores? Or trees? What if the lake got a lot bigger? The blue water would cover everything. It would be a big mess! And what if that happened every year?

People would not live there, would they? They would move away from the lake. They would live in houses that were far away from the lake. They would continue to visit the lake, and they would drive to the lake. But they would not live next to the lake.

But the people of Kompong Luong know they cannot do that. They need the lake. They fish for food, and they sell fish too. The people of Kompong Luong do not have cars. They have only boats. They cannot drive to work. They have to physically stay near the lake to pursue the fish.

Chapter 2
A Lot of Fish!

Tonlé Sap is very important to the country of Cambodia. The lake is in the middle of the country, and it is one of the best neighborhoods in the world to fish. Hundreds of different kinds of fish live in the lake. That's a lot of fish!

People in Cambodia eat fish and rice almost every day. The people could not live without fish. It is their most important food. It keeps them fit. It keeps them strong and at healthy weights. The many millions of fish from Tonlé Sap continue to feed almost all the people in Cambodia.

All those fish must be caught. Many people in Kompong Luong catch fish to feed the country. Their mothers and fathers fished. Their grandparents fished. Now they and their neighbors fish. Their children will probably fish too. It is their way of life. It's also the way they make money and pay their dues.

But where can these fishers live? That is the issue that outweighs all other problems. They have to live near geography that allows them to fish. They have to live on the land right next to the lake. This land is the shore. But the Tonlé Sap shore moves and changes. People cannot live there.

What if they lived on the shore when it rains? The rain falls hard for nearly six months, from May to October. The lake is big then. Finally the rain stops. The lake shrinks, and the shore moves. The people are now miles from the lake, and they cannot pursue the fish.

What if they lived on the shore in April? That is the phase when it does not rain. The lake is smaller. Then the rain starts, and the lake grows. The shore moves. Their neighborhood homes are now under the water. That is not good! What do the people do?

Chapter 3
Living on a Boat

How would you solve the problem of Tonlé Sap? Would you move your house twice a year? That is a big job. About ten thousand people live in Kompong Luong. It is hard to move one house. It is very hard to move houses for ten thousand people in a huge neighborhood!

You could put wheels on the houses to make moving easier. But it would still be hard. Each family would also need to own a piece of land for when it rains and a piece for when the lake shrinks. Only rich people could do that. The Kompong Luong people are very poor.

Long ago the people of Kompong Luong found an answer. They found a way to move with the lake. Here's a clue: Are their houses on wheels? No. Their houses are boats. Their school is a boat, and their stores are boats. Their churches are boats. The whole town floats.

Phenomenally, the people sleep on their houseboats. They also fish from their boats. Children play on the boats. The houseboats have smaller boats tied to them. The smaller boats are like cars. People go to the store in the smaller boats, and the children go to school in them.

There are many floating towns on Tonlé Sap. Kompong Luong is just one of the towns, but it is the largest. It is also very pretty. People take photographs of the town. But it still has issues. Think about it. Can you guess what some problems are?

Chapter 4
Town Problems

Pretend you are going to Kompong Luong. First you fly on a big airplane to a big city. Then you take a smaller airplane to a smaller city. Then someone drives you on a very long road. The trees are tall and green, and the sun is shining in a blue sky. You finally arrive at the lake. It is very pretty.

You take a small boat out to Kompong Luong. The neighborhood boats float quietly on the lake. The sun sparkles on the water. Women wear bright colors. They wear red and purple. They wear blue and yellow. Waterbirds fly across the sky. It is a very pretty picture.

Now look more closely. People are working very hard. They look tired. Many of the children wear old, torn clothes. People are putting trash into the lake. But they also drink the water from the lake, and the dirty water makes people sick. The houseboats have no electricity.

Life continues to be hard in Kompong Luong. The people are very poor. Some have lived there for a long time. Other families once had farms. They lost their land because of a war. Some people came from other countries. The people agree. They don't like living on boats.

The people say their goal is to live on land. They want nice houses and gardens. They want clean water to drink. They want electricity. They want a better school. They want a doctor's office. But they still want to pursue fishing. And Cambodia needs the fish they catch.

The boats solved a big problem. But the boats also caused other problems. The people are looking for new answers now. They are lucky because they have a lot of help. People all over the world are thinking about Kompong Luong. They want to make life in this neighborhood better.

Chapter 5
How to Fix It

People from other countries want to help Kompong Luong. They also want to help clean the lake. There are too many people living on the lake. Due to this lifestyle, the lake is getting very dirty, and the fish are not as healthy as they used to be. Even some of the beautiful waterbirds are starting to die.

The people who live on the boats use wood for fires. They need fires to cook with, but they have cut down too many trees. That hurts the forest and geography around Tonlé Sap. The birds that lived in the trees are dying. Dirt is washing into the lake.

There seems to be only one way to help the lake. There seems to be only one way to help the people. The people must live in houses and neighborhoods on the land. It is the same old issue. Can new people find a new answer? What kind of answer will it be? Can you think of a way to solve the problem?

One answer might be to try to keep the lake small all year. The Cambodians could build dams and walls to keep the lake small. But this might not work. The water could break the dams, and the walls could crumble from the weight. It could also be a catastrophe for the fish because they wouldn't get fresh, clean water.

Another answer might be to find a new place for the people to live. What if people could live away from the Tonlé Sap lake but could still continue to come back to fish? There are plans to make a new river. It would go from the shore of Tonlé Sap to a hill nearby. People could live on the hill and still get the fish they need to survive.

The fishers could keep their fishing boats in the river. Then they could ride in their boats to Tonlé Sap every day. The families could live in a real house with electricity and clean water. They could have a good school and a good doctor. Life would be much better in Kompong Luong.

NOMADS:
People on the Move

By
Chandler Tyrrell

Illustrated by
Arvis Stewart

Columbus, OH

Photo Credits

Cover, Back Cover ©Jim Zuckerman/CORBIS.

SRAonline.com

 SRA

Copyright © 2005 by SRA/McGraw-Hill.

All rights reserved. Except as permitted under the United States Copyright Act, no part of this publication may be reproduced or distributed in any form or by any means, or stored in a database or retrieval system, without the prior written permission of the publisher, unless otherwise indicated.

Send all inquiries to:
SRA/McGraw-Hill
8787 Orion Place
Columbus, OH 43240-4027

Printed in the United States of America.

ISBN 0-07-604468-8

4 5 6 7 8 9 MAL 10 09

Contents

Chapter 1
The Changpa.. 1

Chapter 2
The Machiguenga 6

Chapter 3
The Nenetses 12

Chapter 4
The Bedouins.. 18

Chapter 5
The Masai 23

Chapter 1
The Changpa

Early humans did not know how to cultivate crops or how to raise animals for food. In order to survive, they roamed from place to place to find food. They hunted animals and found berries and plants to eat. Eventually, humans learned how to cultivate crops and how to raise animals on farms for food. Cities formed near farms, and people began to stay in one place. Today, most people move only a few times in their lifetimes.

Yet there are still some people in the world who move a lot from place to place. These people are nomads. Nomads do not have just one home. They live in different places at different times of the year. Each group of nomads continues to move around for different reasons.

The Changpa are nomads in India in the Himalayas. The Himalayas are mountains. The Changpa have learned how to raise animals and herd goats, sheep, and yaks. These animals graze, which means they eat grass. But grass doesn't grow well in the mountains; the ground is rocky and dry. So even though the Changpa have learned how to raise animals, they still need to move around frequently, looking for new grazing grass.

Yak hair helps the Changpa in many ways. The Changpa live in *rebos,* which are tents woven from yak hair. Yak hair is also used to make carpets and ropes, and yak milk is used to make cheese, yogurt, and butter. Yak droppings are burned to make fires for cooking and heating. Yaks also help the Changpa move by carrying overweight things on their backs from place to place.

Changpa sheep have wool called cashmere. After the wool has been cut off the sheep, the Changpa people travel to the city to sell the wool at the markets for money. Then the Changpa go back into the mountains to travel again. People buy the wool to weave into blankets and clothing that are of great value.

Chapter 2
The Machiguenga

The Machiguenga live in Manu National Park in Peru. Some of them live outside the park and work for wood, oil, or coffee companies. Others continue to live the way the Machiguenga people have lived for hundreds of years. The Machiguenga are nomads who hunt, fish, and cultivate crops.

Manu National Park is a huge area. Rain forest covers most of the park, and there are many writhing rivers. The Machiguenga people set up their towns near the rivers and streams in the forest so they have a way to travel. They use the water to float boats and travel places.

Machiguenga families have more than one home because of the wet and dry seasons. Families live one place during the wet season when it rains a lot, which helps their crops grow. The biggest crop is manioc. It's like a potato. During the dry season when it doesn't rain as much and the Machiguenga's food and crops won't grow, they live in towns where there are schools for children to learn to read and write.

During the dry season when the rivers are low, the Machiguenga move again to another neighborhood. Families camp along these rivers, where fish are easier to catch, and turtle eggs can be found in the soil. When the dry season ends, it's time to move back to the town near the schools for children to learn to read and write. Later, the Machiguenga will move back to their farms during the wet season.

In order to cultivate crops, part of the forest has to be cut and burned to make a field. This isn't wrong—burning the soil actually makes the soil healthy because it replaces nutrients that help plants grow. After two or three years, the soil is no longer healthy and cannot grow any more crops. The Machiguenga have to make a new field in another place.

Women work in the fields during the wet season. They use their hands and wrists to gather and load up wild fruits and nuts from the forest for food. One popular snack is ice-cream beans. They are sweet white nuts. Beetle grubs are also eaten. People say they taste like peanut butter! While the women farm, the men hunt for meat or fish.

Chapter 3
The Nenetses

In the far north of Russia in Siberia, the Nenetses travel across the tundra. Tundra is found in the coldest parts of the world. Very few trees or plants grow there because the tundra ground is frozen most of the year. The Nenetses move as the seasons change because the location of the best food for their reindeer changes with the seasons.

Reindeer are very important to the Nenets people. Reindeer give the people many things of value that help them live. Warm clothing and tents called *chums* are made from reindeer skin. The Nenetses also get most of what they eat from the reindeer, by using many parts of the reindeer.

In the summer, the tundra is not as cold, and the reindeer like to eat lichen, which is like a plant and grows on the tundra's rocks. Reindeer have special hooves like sharp, thick toenails. The hooves help dig into ice to keep the reindeer from slipping on the frozen tundra ground as they search for lichen. There are hundreds of reindeer, and all the lichen in an area is eaten in a short time. Then the Nenetses must roam to a new area.

The *chums* the Nenetses live in look like tepees. Inside, a wood fire burns. Furs are on the *chum* walls and keep out the cold. Nenetses drink hot tea to keep themselves warm. The tea is made from loads of clean, melted snow.

When winter arrives, the Nenets nomads move south. They take down their camp and then wrap it up and put everything in the camp onto wooden sleds. Reindeer pull the weight on the sleds to warmer places. In the south, the tundra has more trees. This area also has animals and plants for the Nenetses.

When the adults move south in winter with the reindeer, the children stay behind to go to school. Some children also visit parts of the world that have telephones and electricity, but most choose to remain where they were born and continue living the life of the nomad.

Chapter 4
The Bedouins

Bedouins live in the desert and travel in some of the driest arid lands on Earth. They move across the Arabian and North African deserts. These Arab nomads survive by herding camels, goats, and sheep. Bedouins roam in search of water and good grazing areas. In this harsh land, such an oasis is very hard to find.

Bedouins wear long, loose robes. They wrap scarves around their heads and faces. Their clothes keep away the hot sun and the strong winds of the desert. Bedouin tents are partly made of goat or camel hair. Inside the tents, Bedouins stay cool during the summer and warm during the winter.

During the hottest part of summer, Bedouin families stay in one place because it's too hot and too risky to cross the desert. Some families live in cities because they want to be near water. But when the weather gets cooler, Bedouins load up their things and move across the desert as they have always done.

Each Bedouin group travels inside its own large area. Piles of stones mark a group's land. Bedouins watch for the piles and don't travel into another group's area. This way, Bedouins respect each other's privacy and land.

Camels are the Bedouins' most important animals. Camels can go days without water in the desert and can carry a lot of weight too.

Life in the desert is difficult, and Bedouins are usually one of the only groups of people living there. For this reason, Bedouins don't meet other travelers very often. If Bedouins do have visitors to their camp, they treat the visitors as special guests and invite them inside their tents. The Bedouins give their guests tea, coffee, and food. Bedouins are good hosts and remain friendly even in the harsh desert.

Chapter 5
The Masai

The Masai people live on the plains of the African savanna. A savanna is an area that is covered in grass. The Masai have lived in this grassland for hundreds of years. They are nomads who travel with herds of cows. The Masai roam across the land, looking for the best grazing spots.

A Masai town is called an *enkang*. The houses in the town are placed in a circle. The houses are shaped a little like igloos. Masai women make the houses from things found in the savanna: sticks, grass, and cow droppings. There are piles of thorns around the town to keep out foes and wild animals.

The savanna has many grassy plains. But if the Masai stay in one place too long, woefully their cows eat all the grass. The Masai must move to a new area so that the plains they leave behind have a chance to grow back. The Masai can return after the grass has grown again.

The Masai women and girls work in the town while the Masai men and boys herd the animals. Animals are a very important part of the Masai way of life. The Masai get milk and meat from their animals. The Masai also sell their animals to other people to get money.

The Masai herd goats and sheep. They used to trade these animals with others, but cows are now the most important animals. Today the Masai sometimes sell cows for money. The more animals a family has, the more money the family gets. Selling cows for money is changing the way the families live.

Like all nomads, the Masai have less and less land to live on, because the modern world is using the land for other things. Much Masai land has been made into parks. People also approach and search for oil in the ground there. Woefully, the way of life for many nomads is ending.

By
Linda Barr

Illustrated by
Kristen Goeters

Columbus, OH

The **McGraw·Hill** Companies

Photo Credits

Cover, Back Cover ©Roger Ressmeyer/CORBIS.

SRAonline.com

 SRA

Copyright © 2005 by SRA/McGraw-Hill.

All rights reserved. Except as permitted under the United States Copyright Act, no part of this publication may be reproduced or distributed in any form or by any means, or stored in a database or retrieval system, without the prior written permission of the publisher, unless otherwise indicated.

Send all inquiries to:
SRA/McGraw-Hill
8787 Orion Place
Columbus, OH 43240-4027

Printed in the United States of America.

ISBN 0-07-604469-6

3 4 5 6 7 8 9 MAL 10 09 08 07 06

Contents

Chapter 1
Earthquake! 1

Chapter 2
A Whole Lot of Shaking 6

Chapter 3
Problems, Problems 12

Chapter 4
What Works 18

Chapter 5
Earthquakes Are Everywhere 23

Chapter 1
Earthquake!

"Why is the ground shaking?" Carlos asked.

He was sitting on a blanket with his cousins Hilda and Julia, his grandma, and his grandpa. They were having the nicest picnic at a park.

"It's an earthquake!" his grandma yelled. "Let's get away from these trees."

They rushed to a field.

Carlos lived in Missouri. He hadn't visited California in the longest time; this was his first earthquake. He would remember this visit for a long time!

The ground continued to shake. Carlos thought it would never stop. His grandma was hugging him, Hilda, and Julia tighter and tighter, but he was still scared!

Finally the earthquake was over, and they heard fire trucks. Carlos and his family hurried home, but driving wasn't easy. Some streets and buildings had the biggest cracks he'd ever seen.

A few porches had fallen down. Some people had come outside so nothing could fall on them inside. No one seemed to be hurt.

At last they turned onto his grandparents' street. Hilda yelled, "Your house is all right!"

Carlos was glad about that, but he was also puzzled. Why were some houses all right while others were destroyed? How could the same earthquake crack some buildings and not hurt others?

That night the TV showed pictures of parts of the town that had been hit the nastiest. Again, Carlos saw that other buildings weren't damaged at all.

"Are some buildings stronger than others?" he asked.

"I can explain that," his grandpa said. "First I will tell you about earthquakes. I just need a hard-boiled egg."

Chapter 2
A Whole Lot of Shaking

His grandpa found an egg in the kitchen. He tapped it softly, and the shell cracked.

"Earth is covered with a rocky shell," he explained. "Earth's shell is cracked like this egg, but those cracks are very deep underground. Earth's shell has about twelve main pieces called plates."

"These plates move very slowly," his grandpa told them. "They push against each other."

He held his hands out flat and said, "Imagine my hands are Earth's plates." Then he pushed his hands together harder and harder.

"Watch out! A lot of energy is building up," he said.

Suddenly his grandpa let one hand slide under the other.

"When the plates slide, they move the ground above them," he said. "We call it an earthquake. Some earthquakes are very small. We don't even feel the slightest shake. Others shake the ground really hard, and buildings fall down."

"But why do some buildings fall down and others don't?" Carlos asked.

"Well, do you remember what happened when Julia threw a stone into the pond at the park?" his grandma asked him.

Carlos nodded and said, "The stone made waves that spread out in bigger and bigger circles."

"Earthquakes send out waves too," his grandma said. "These waves are made of energy, not water. The first waves push the ground from side to side, and the next waves push the ground up and down. All this shaking can damage anything built on that ground!"

"But why does shaking damage just some buildings?" Carlos asked.

"We have found ways to keep buildings from falling down," his grandma explained. She was an engineer and helped plan new buildings. "We've learned many things about dealing with earthquakes."

"What's the neatest thing you've learned?" Julia asked.

Chapter 3
Problems, Problems

"First, no building is really 'earthquake proof,'" his grandma said. "A very strong earthquake can damage any building. It can cause any bridge to fall. It can crack any road."

Carlos shook his head and thought about going back to Missouri. He had never felt an earthquake there!

"Still, some buildings are damaged by the smallest quakes. Many of those buildings are made of concrete," his grandma said. "Concrete is like the cement in sidewalks. Concrete makes buildings stronger—and stiffer.

"Earthquakes jerk buildings," she said. "A concrete building can't bend or sway. It just cracks."

Carlos thought about the damaged buildings he had seen. A few of them did look like piles of cement chunks.

"Now builders put long steel rods in the concrete," his grandma said. "The rods make the buildings stronger. Then the buildings can bend just a little without cracking."

"Bending too much can also be a problem," his grandma said. "For example, a wide roof, such as a gym roof, should not bend easily. An earthquake can make a wide roof flop up and down. Then the roof might cave in."

Building in California was not easy!

Hilda said, "What about that office building we saw on TV? It was wood and didn't have a wide roof. It still fell down."

"Its first floor was a garage, which has lots of open space," his grandma said. "The garage couldn't hold up the floors above it."

"Now we make garages stronger," his grandma said. "We also try to build on rock. Rock soaks up some of an earthquake's nastiest energy. If a house is built on soft soil, the soil can turn into liquid in an earthquake!"

Carlos stared at his toes on the floor. Was his grandparents' house built on rock?

Chapter 4
What Works

"We have found more ways to keep buildings from shaking too," his grandma said. "One way is to put layers of rubber and steel under buildings. The quake hits these layers first. The layers soak up some of its unsafe energy. Then the building does not shake so much."

"Some buildings have a special base that slides," his grandma told them.

She drew two buildings and showed what would happen in an earthquake. One unstable building swayed back and forth, but the other building had a sliding base. If an earthquake hit, only the base would sway.

"How do you know what works?" Carlos asked.

"We put instruments in many buildings," his grandma explained. "The instruments tell how much each building moves during an earthquake. We know if the building moves up and down, side to side, or both. After a quake, we check for unfortunate damage."

"We see how well each kind of building does in a quake," his grandma said. "That tells us what works and what's unsuccessful."

Just then, a man on TV said no one else was trapped in any buildings. Still, Carlos saw some workers poking around in the hardest-hit buildings.

"They are trying to find out why each unsteady building cracked or fell," his grandpa said. "That helps us understand what works and what doesn't."

"Well, I'm glad we don't have any earthquakes in Missouri!" Carlos said.

His grandpa smiled and asked, "Have you ever heard of New Madrid?"

Chapter 5
Earthquakes Are Everywhere

"New Madrid is in Missouri. It's south of the town where you live," his grandpa said. "This town had one of our country's biggest earthquakes."

His grandma nodded. "It was really three big quakes. They were in 1811 and 1812. Unbelievably, the first one shook the ground over hundreds of miles."

"That first earthquake rang church bells in Boston," his grandma said. "That's a thousand miles away! It made part of the Mississippi River run backward!"

"The unsafe earthquakes knocked down whole towns," his grandpa said. "Nothing could stand up to earthquakes back then."

Maybe Carlos should stay in California!

"I thought only California had earthquakes," Julia said.

"No, Alaska has the highest number of quakes of all the states," his grandma said. "California has the second-most earthquakes, but many other states have earthquakes too. They are all caused by Earth's unstable plates pushing on one another."

"Will New Madrid ever have another quake?" Carlos asked. "Will it make my town fall down?"

"Actually, earthquakes still do happen near New Madrid. However, people are trying to make sure they aren't unprepared," his grandma said. "They are learning more about Earth's plates in that area."

"Now I remember that we had some earthquake drills at school in the uncomfortable basement," Carlos said. "I had never been in an earthquake before. Now I know why the drills are important!"

Hilda smiled and said, "We have earthquake drills at school all the time." She smiled wider. "Some of them are for real!"

Carlos shook his head. "I have learned more about Missouri by coming to California! I know more about safer buildings now too."

His grandma nodded and gave her grandson a hug. "Maybe you will become an engineer someday. Then you can plan unbreakable buildings that help save people's lives!"

Stuck in the Snow

By
Hilary Mac Austin

Illustrated by
Angela Adams

Columbus, OH

Photo Credits

Cover, Back Cover ©Tom Bean/CORBIS;
11 ©Frank Cezus/Getty Images, Inc.

SRAonline.com

 SRA

Copyright © 2005 by SRA/McGraw-Hill.

All rights reserved. Except as permitted under the United States Copyright Act, no part of this publication may be reproduced or distributed in any form or by any means, or stored in a database or retrieval system, without the prior written permission of the publisher, unless otherwise indicated.

Send all inquiries to:
SRA/McGraw-Hill
8787 Orion Place
Columbus, OH 43240-4027

Printed in the United States of America.

ISBN 0-07-604470-X

5 6 7 8 9 MAL 10 09

Contents

Chapter 1
Going to the Canyon 1

Chapter 2
The Storm Hits 9

Chapter 3
Be Prepared 19

Chapter 4
Dinner in the Car 29

Chapter 5
Saved! 36

Chapter 1
Going to the Canyon

Nikki Sutherly is excited, and her younger brother Alexander is too. The Sutherly children are on their first trip ever! It's spring break, and they're on a camping trip. They've been driving for a few days and playing games, and today they will ultimately arrive at the campsite.

The Sutherlys are going to camp near the Grand Canyon. Nikki is ten, and she wants to be a famous scientist when she grows up. Her favorite class in school is earth science. Alexander is eight and wants to be a firefighter—just like his mom and dad.

The Sutherlys are almost at the Grand Canyon. They're driving up the steepest mountain roads they've ever seen. On one side of the road are vertical cliffs dropping into huge canyons. Nikki can see for miles. The blue sky is enormous, but there are dark clouds gathering on the horizon.

Dad looks uneasily at the threatening clouds. "We should find out about the weather," he says. He turns on the radio and finds a weather report.

"Hey, folks," says the weather reporter cheerily, "it seems an unexpected storm is moving in from the north. Welcome to spring in northern Arizona!"

Nikki and Alexander are ecstatic. They've never seen snow before. Alexander bounces on the backseat, and Mom and Dad glance at each other. "Do you think we should turn around?" asks Mom.

"Well, we're more than halfway there. It will take longer if we turn and go back," Dad says softly.

He looks in the rearview mirror and in a louder voice says, "Anyway, it's only twenty more miles. We'll be there in no time."

Alexander and Nikki whoop with happiness. Snow *and* the Grand Canyon! Life is fantastic! Nikki looks out the window again, but something seems different.

The shadowy clouds have moved fast, and now they're covering the sun. Only a few minutes ago it was the loveliest sunny spring day, and now everything seems gray and cold. It starts snowing, and Nikki and Alexander gasp. The snowflakes look like feathers tumbling slowly from the sky.

Dad drives more carefully, but soon the road becomes flatter, and they enter a forest. Mom and Dad sigh with relief. They didn't like driving up a mountain in the slippery snow. Nikki doesn't notice—she can't stop staring out the window. "It's so unbelievably beautiful," she whispers.

Chapter 2
The Storm Hits

The gentle snowfall doesn't last long, however. Soon the snowflakes get smaller and fall faster, and the wind begins to blow violently. Dad turns on the headlights, and then the weather reporter comes on again. "Hey, there, folks," he reports, "our innocent spring snowstorm has turned into a real blizzard!"

"You know the rules," he continues. "Get off the road, and get inside. We're getting reports of winds up to . . ." The voice begins to crackle. Soon all they can hear is static. The signal is gone! Mom and Dad look at each other unsmilingly. They're worried. This is serious!

"We'll be okay," Dad says quietly to Mom. She nods and tries to relax. Dad drives slowly, and his face is tense. The car is barely moving as Dad attempts to see where he's going, but all he can see are millions of tiny white snowflakes blustering everywhere!

Dad has to stop the car. He can't continue driving because he can't see the road anymore! Everyone remains quiet. Mom looks at Dad and at Nikki and Alexander. Then Mom smiles and claps her hands rapidly. "Well, it looks like we're camping in the car tonight!" she says.

Dad grins back at Mom. "Sure looks like it," he says. "Aw, this'll be no problem," he adds, looking at Nikki and Alexander. "We're tough firefighters, aren't we?" Dad always says this when he wants Nikki and Alexander to be brave. Nikki wants to be brave, but suddenly she's terrified.

The wind is howling, and Nikki feels cold, small, and unhappy. *How can everyone be so calm?* she thinks as she tries not to cry.

"We have our camping gear," Mom says.

"And you packed enough food for an army," adds Dad.

"And *I* have my adventure kit!" says Alexander proudly.

Mom, Dad, and Nikki all look at Alexander with curiosity. "Your what?" asks Dad.

"My adventure kit," Alexander says happily. "In case we had an adventure." Alexander starts rummaging through his backpack. He removes a compass, a flashlight, batteries, rope, garbage bags, candles, a bright orange scarf, and beef jerky.

"Honey, your adventure kit is going to be such a gigantic help," says Mom.

Nikki feels a little jealous. *Alexander is helping with his silly adventure kit, and he's the youngest. I should be helping too,* she thinks. But she's too frightened to think. She can't remember anything!

"Okay, guys, this car is becoming colder. I think we need to unpack our supplies from the trunk. I'll get them," says Dad.

"I'll help," agrees Mom.

Nikki imagines her parents in the enormous storm and then suddenly remembers something: She has learned about blizzards! How could she forget?

"No! Wait!" shouts Nikki. "Listen, everyone! I know about blizzards. We studied them in school." Everyone stops and looks seriously at her.

"Go on, baby," says Mom slowly.

"Well, the air becomes frigid, and the wind blows really violently," Nikki says quickly. "It's easy to become lost or get frostbite."

Chapter 3
Be Prepared

Nikki is thinking fast now. "First, we need Alexander's rope," she says. "That way, one person can hold on to the other person." They decide Dad will go out and Mom will hold the rope.

"First, Dad, you need to rewrap yourself with more clothes," says Nikki. "It could be below zero outside!"

"Dad, don't go outside!" Alexander cries suddenly. He looks at everyone with wide eyes.

Nikki understands being scared. "It'll be okay, Alexander," she says.

Mom reassures him in her gentlest voice. "These are just adventure rules."

"He'll be safe?" asks Alexander.

"Sure I will!" Dad says confidently. "I promise. Now, hand over your socks, little man!"

Alexander regains his smile, and soon everyone has offered a piece of their clothing.

"Pretty good, Dad," says Nikki, "but you need something to keep you dry in that wet snow. I know! Alexander, we need your garbage bags."

Alexander smiles even wider. "Oh, and here's the flashlight, Dad. You'll need that too," he says proudly.

Then Nikki leans toward the front seat.

"I don't want to frighten Alexander again," she whispers to her parents, "but during our blizzard review, we learned that a blizzard's snow can bury a car. People will be unable to discover us. We need to tie something to the antenna—it's the highest part of the car. People will see it."

"Nikki, I'm so delighted you pay attention in school," Mom whispers back. Then Mom says loudly, "Because this is a real adventure, I think we need a flag. Do you have something in your adventure kit, Alexander?"

"My orange scarf! It'll be a perfect adventure flag!" Alexander says with enthusiasm. The scarf reappears in his hand.

Soon Dad is ready to go. He has Mom's red sweatshirt tied around his neck, Nikki's yellow sweater covering his head and ears, Alexander's socks as mittens, one of Alexander's garbage bags as a raincoat, and the other bags tied over his galoshes. The rope is retied around his waist again and again.

Alexander giggles. "You look absolutely ridiculous, Dad."

"He does, doesn't he?" says Mom, chuckling. "Hold on, I need to find a camera. Your friends at the firehouse will love this!"

"Oh no, you don't." Dad laughs as he grabs Alexander's flashlight and scarf from the backseat and then returns to the front. "I'll never hear the end of it."

"I'll return," Dad says confidently, and then he pushes and pushes on the door. He almost can't open it because the snow is already so unbelievably high! Also, the wind is extremely strong. When he finally gets out of the car, he vanishes into the snow. Mom holds the rope tightly.

Wet snow and freezing air blow through the open door. Dad slowly pushes through the snow and wind, and Mom feeds out the rope. Then Nikki feels the trunk open and close. When Dad returns, he throws sleeping bags and backpacks into the car.

"One more trip," he gasps.

Again Dad vanishes. Mom refeeds the rope, and Nikki feels the trunk open and close. Finally Dad plunks a cooler and a shovel into the car, and then he awkwardly climbs in and shuts the door. He's covered in so much snow! He looks like a friendly snowman with outrageous clothing.

Chapter 4
Dinner in the Car

"Grab the shovel, Alexander," Mom orders. "Nikki, grab this cooler. Okay, time for a little heat." She turns on the car, unties the rope, and rips the wet garbage bags off Dad. Nikki has never seen anyone move quite so fast, but Mom is so calm and reassured! Everyone watches.

"Nikki, toss me a sleeping bag," says Mom. Then she rubs Dad's feet and hands. "Wiggle your toes, Nate," she says to Dad.

Dad envelops himself in a sleeping bag. The car is quickly getting much warmer, and the crystal snow melts off Dad's face. "Wow," he says, "that was really amazing!"

"Okay, kids," Dad says, "what do you think we should do now?"

Alexander and Nikki talk at the same time. "We should put on all our clothes," says Nikki, while Alexander shouts, "I'm hungry!"

Mom laughs merrily. "Both are very good ideas, but let's put on some more clothes first."

The Sutherlys put on all their clothes and crawl into their sleeping bags. They look quite cozy.

"Alexander, I believe we need your adventure kit again," Mom says. "We'll need the light from your candles when Dad turns off the car."

"Candles also will help keep the car from getting too uncomfortably cold," adds Nikki.

"But, Mom, what are we going to put the candles into?" asks Alexander.

"I know!" says Nikki. "Mom, do you have any empty cups?"

"Fantastic idea, Nikki," says Mom. "I have our metal camping cups somewhere." Soon the candles are safely lit, and there is the prettiest flickering light in the car.

"Okay, everyone, get ready because I'm turning off the car. We need to save the gasoline," says Dad.

Then Mom starts to open her window!

"*No!*" cry Alexander and Nikki. "It's too cold, Mom!"

"I know it's cold," says Mom. "But candles burn oxygen, and we need fresh air."

"Now, who wants dinner?" says Mom.

"I do!" Alexander and Nikki holler happily from inside their sleeping bags.

Mom makes sandwiches, Alexander gives everyone some of his beef jerky, and they drink apple juice from the cooler. It feels satisfying to be full of food, but everyone is now freezing.

Chapter 5
Saved!

"I think we need to warm up a little bit," Dad says.

Whew, Dad is going to turn on the heat! thinks Nikki.

But instead Dad says, "Come on, everybody, let's get moving! Wiggle your bodies!" He starts singing. Soon they're all singing and wiggling in their sleeping bags.

The dancing and singing work. Everyone is warmer, and Mom blows out the candles and closes the window a bit. "Bedtime," she says. Nikki and Alexander snuggle in their sleeping bags and soon are sleeping soundly. Mom and Dad stay awake all night to make sure their children remain safe and unhurt.

The next morning Nikki is startled by a loud noise. Dad is honking the horn! Nikki pops her head out of the sleeping bag. Sunshine is pouring into the car through the tops of the windows. The car is nearly covered by the unrelenting snow.

Why is Dad honking? she wonders curiously.

She hears yelling from outside. Hooray! Help has arrived! Nikki is unbelievably happy. She shakes Alexander. Suddenly she hears someone walking on the roof of the car. Then she sees feet walking next to the top of Mom's window! The feet are walking on top of the snow! The person leans over.

The friendly face of a park ranger appears in Mom's window.

"Well, look what we have here," the ranger says. "Is everyone okay?"

"Are we glad to see you!" says Mom with relief. "We're all fine, but we'd love to get out of this car!"

The ranger laughs. "I can understand that!"

The ranger shovels snow away from Mom's window. Soon the window can open all the way. One by one, the Sutherlys crawl out the window and stand in the bright sunshine. Alexander plays and falls in the deep snow. Nikki just stares at the bright white blanket of snow everywhere.

The ranger looks at the sky. "This storm caught everyone by surprise. We've been digging out people all morning. I almost missed you, but I saw the scarf on your antenna and returned. And you kept a window open. Both are really intelligent moves. You really know your blizzard survival rules."

"We've never seen snow before," says Dad. He points to Alexander and Nikki and adds, "Our kids were unafraid and had all the answers."

"We used my adventure kit!" says Alexander happily.

"Wow, I've never heard of an adventure kit," says the ranger. "You'll have to tell me everything about it."

The ranger carries Alexander to her snowmobile. Alexander chatters the entire way, telling and retelling the ranger all about his adventure kit. The ranger nods and smiles at the small boy. Mom and Dad give Nikki a hug.

"I'm so proud of you," Mom whispers into Nikki's ear. "You saved our lives!"